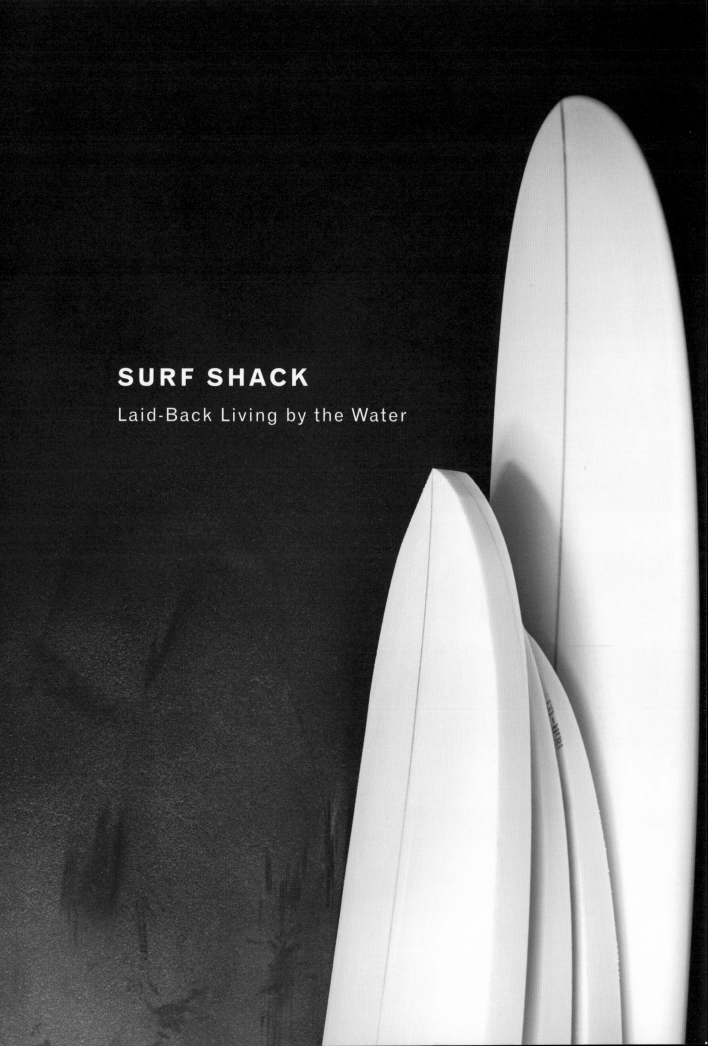

SURF SHACK

Laid-Back Living by the Water

SURF SHACK

Laid-Back Living by the Water

Nina Freudenberger

WITH HEATHER SUMMERVILLE

PHOTOGRAPHS BY Brittany Ambridge

CLARKSON POTTER/PUBLISHERS
NEW YORK

Copyright © 2017 by Nina Freudenberger

Photographs copyright © 2017 by
Brittany Ambridge

All rights reserved.

Published in the United States by Clarkson
Potter/Publishers, an imprint of the Crown
Publishing Group, a division of Penguin
Random House LLC, New York.
crownpublishing.com
clarksonpotter.com

CLARKSON POTTER is a trademark and
POTTER with colophon is a registered
trademark of Penguin Random House LLC.

Library of Congress Cataloging-in-
Publication Data has been applied for.

ISBN 978-0-451-49605-8

eBook ISBN 978-0-451-49606-5

Printed in China

Interior and cover design by
Stephanie Huntwork
Interior and cover photographs by
Brittany Ambridge

10 9 8 7 6 5

First Edition

For Mike & Wolf

CONTENTS

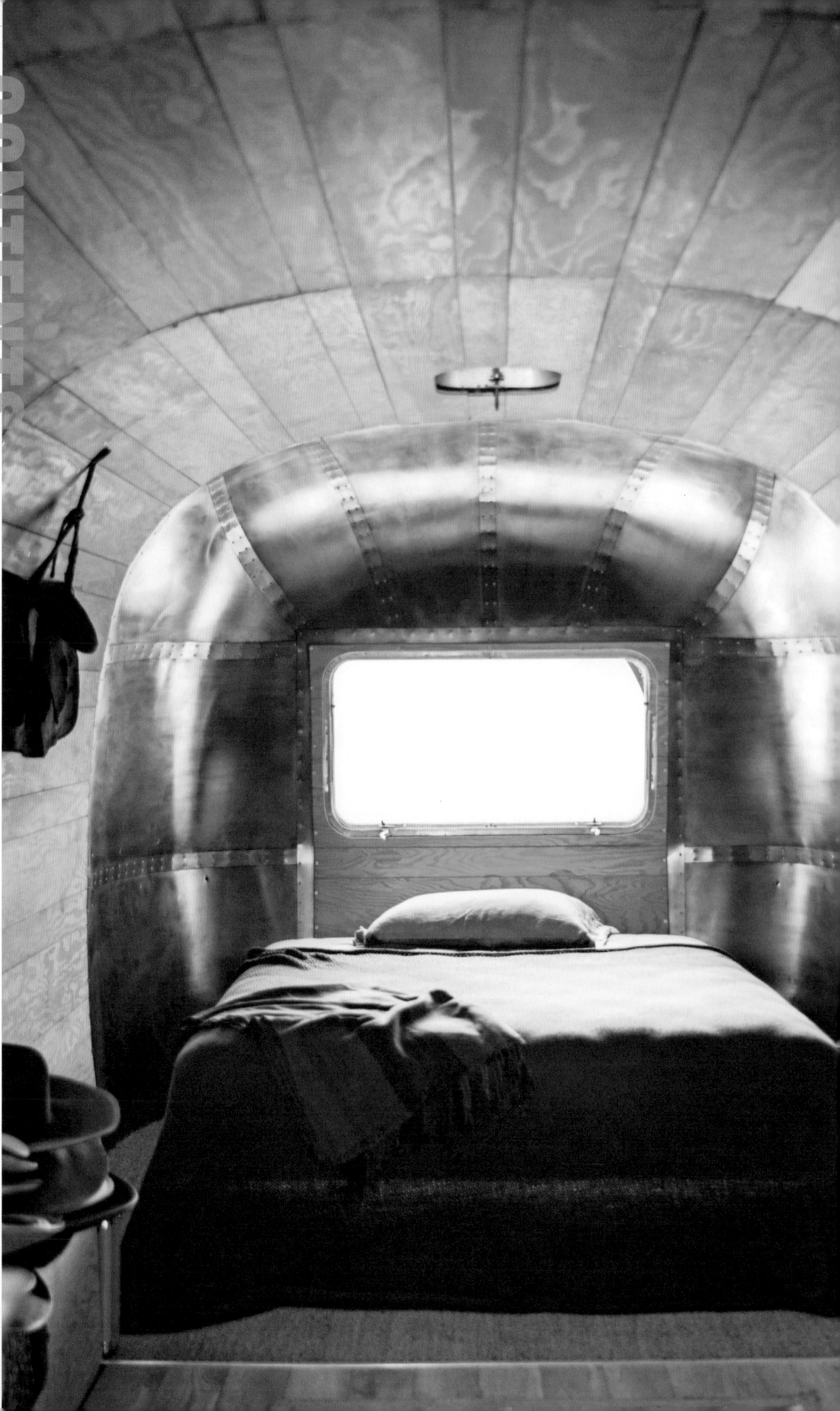

INTRODUCTION

WHEN I MOVED FROM NEW YORK CITY TO VENICE, CALIFORNIA, IN 2012 I never expected the getting-to-work part of my day to look quite so different. All of a sudden everything I ever pictured a morning commute to be was turned inside out—it was untucked and wearing flip-flops. No longer was I sharing a sidewalk with half-frantic business types speed-walking to their first meetings. Instead, morning after morning, I watched as my new neighbors meandered their way to the beach with surfboards strapped to bicycles, belted to cars, or tucked under arms. The contradiction was fascinating.

As I met more people on the West Coast, hung out in their homes, and had dinner with their families, I discovered that a lot of them were surfers. And what's more, surfing wasn't a recreational activity they happen to enjoy; it was more of a calling, a way of life that washed through every other aspect of their world. These folks were happy, they were relaxed, and their homes echoed those traits. Clearly they are doing something right in life—and I wanted to get to the how and why of it all.

To take on the monstrous task of writing about surfing, though, is like landing in a foreign country for the first time. The surf world has its own rules. It has its own language, its own rich history, its own style. It does not tolerate outsiders gladly. But navigating the unwritten laws of the water wasn't the thing that interested me. I didn't want to know about how to work a lineup or avoiding localism; that's not what this book is about. Instead, as an interior designer, I became endlessly intrigued by the culture itself, and the "surf shacks" that these wave riders returned to after a day on the water.

So, I decided to go exploring. I traveled to eighteen cities in four countries; I hung out with a lot of surfers who had been riding their whole lives, and others who were just starting out. I met a board-collecting Brooklyn couple who willingly starts their day at 5 a.m. with a two-hour round-trip to the nearest beach in order to fit in a pre-work surf session. I spoke with a West Coast family who uprooted their city lives for a more remote location just so their son can grow up in the sort of tight-knit community that surfers seem to cultivate.

Here's what I learned: Surfing is a natural filter for life's nonsense. It requires discipline, focus, and patience—and I'm not strictly talking about what happens in the water. People who make surfing a priority don't have a lot of room to get caught up in the day-to-day noise that disorients the rest of us. It takes effort and time to surf; there's the lugging of equipment, the commute to the beach, the uncertainty of whether Mother Nature is even going to cooperate. By default, this community has mastered a sort of life-work-surf balance that keeps their world blissfully streamlined.

And that sentiment spills over into the homes they create for themselves, which are less about impressive architecture and more about cultivating truly authentic spaces. All of the rooms you see in this book prioritize ease over elegance, good vibes over any sort of grand vision. These are not flawless residences with unwaxed surfboards mounted on walls as decoration; they are unbuttoned and covered in sand. Spaces become whatever they need to be: bedrooms double as home offices, abandoned aviaries serve as surfboard lockers, throw pillows are passable seating. These homes are flexible and relaxed, a perfect snapshot of the people who live in them.

Just as these natural risk-takers are rewriting the rules of decorating, they're also redefining the idea of what work looks like. So many surfers I met are artists and designers, chefs and shopkeepers, photographers and filmmakers—and their job

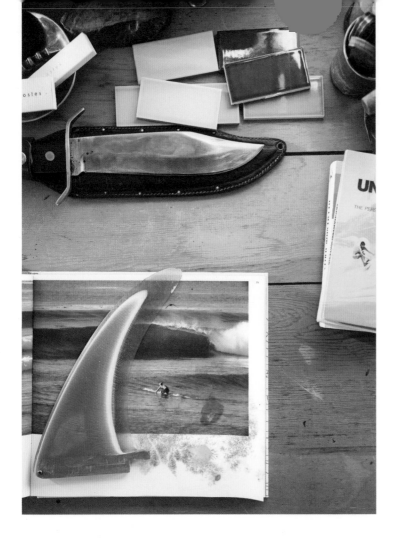

titles are often a combination of one or two or more of these professions. Whether surfing begets creativity or vice versa is tough to say. But it's abundantly clear that there is a natural intuition and self-reliance among riders, one that allows them the freedom to successfully thrive outside of a nine-to-five job.

All of this gets to the heart of what makes this way of life so damn charming. A surf shack is not built around what you think you need, so much as it is about understanding all the things you don't. You don't need a house directly on the ocean or even a ton of money. Have the courage to go your own way. Be confident in your decisions. Find magic in life's little imperfections. These are the traits I saw over and over again in the people I met—and they are the traits, I think, that make for a happy life . . . whatever that happens to look like.

If I've learned nothing else on this adventure it's this: Create a home around something you love doing, and it can't help but be beautiful.

HANG

the
newbies

MIDCENTURY RANCH

Andrea Shaw and Duncan Russell-Smith
Torquay, Australia

EVERY SURFER HAS A VERSION OF *THAT* STORY. THE ONE ABOUT their perfect wave or the best day they've ever had on the water. Most of these tales involve double or triple overheads, or paddling out in some far-flung locale. But that's not the case for Aussie artist Andrea Shaw. Her idea of a good time is far more simple than that: A great day at her favorite local break Point Roadknight. "If there's a big enough swell, you can get this really long beautiful ride," says Andrea. "You can literally catch a wave, take it five hundred meters or so to shore, walk back to the break on the beach, and start the whole circuit all over again."

It doesn't hurt, of course, that Andrea lives in one of the best surf towns on the planet. Torquay is where legendary brands like Quicksilver and Rip Curl are headquartered. But it's still a telling portrait of her mellow, in-it-for-the-ride approach. Andrea started surfing just three years ago and, initially, only got into it to have a more accessible alternative to skiing and snowboarding, which she's been doing since she was five years old. "For some reason, I have this obsessive need to propel myself over the Earth at high speeds," she laughs. It's a passion, though, and the fact that she could only afford to snowboard once a year was taking its toll.

So she's been filling that void with surfing, hitting the water far more often than she ever saw the slopes. Unlike most newbies, though, Andrea never took a single lesson. Instead she

PREVIOUS PAGE
Bondi Beach, Sydney

ACROSS Nirvana was still touring the last time this kitchen saw an update. Instead of masking the nineties vibe, Andrea went with it, bringing in dish towels and artwork (both her own designs) covered in patterns and colors indicative of that decade.

Colorful stacks of vintage textiles are stashed all over this house (from African wax prints to hand-stitched quilts), all of which get tossed across beds or draped over sofas whenever the need to change up the mood of a room strikes.

Andrea is what you'd call a surfboard minimalist: She has a longboard (snagged off a local used-board Facebook group), and a shortboard (seen here), which is a custom design by shaper Corey Graham that she hand-painted.

A lack of funds never hampers this couple's eclectic style; if anything, it eggs them on to be more creative with how they use what they have. In the living room, for instance, handwoven objects from Cook Islands are hung as art.

bought a board and went at it trial-and-error style, saying the only thing she ever really worries about are run-ins with the old sea dogs who've been surfing the same breaks for forty years. "Get in their way or snake one of their waves, and it's like your grandpa giving you a talking-to."

Localism be damned, at least once a week, she paddles out with a group of ladies she rides with, many of them fellow artists and creatives who work out of the same studio as Andrea and her furniture-making husband, Duncan Russell-Smith. "The group texts start before sunrise. We don't even use words anymore, just emojis: Surf emoji. Thumbs-up emoji. Thumbs-down emoji. Question mark," she says. "That's standard practice—even in the winter." All the members of her crew surf because it's fun. Being in nature, on the water, is peaceful, relaxing, and centering for them.

It was this need to be outdoors that brought Andrea and Duncan to the Surf Coast three years ago. He's originally from

ACROSS AND ABOVE
In addition to amazing surf, Torquay is home to some of the best trails around. Once a week, Andrea and Duncan (with a very happy Tilly in tow) hike the cliffside paths that connect one beach to the next along the Great Ocean Road.

ABOVE After designing textiles for years, Andrea turned to painting, applying the same love of color and abstract shapes she once printed on fabrics to a series of works on canvas inspired by her fascination with satellite imagery and digital maps.
ACROSS A bathroom with windows may not top most people's list of home luxuries, but if you ask Andrea, after a morning surf there's nothing better than a hot shower accompanied by a cool breeze.

England, and she grew up on a farm in the country. After years of living in Melbourne together, they were ready for a change that involved a little more house and a lot more greenery—and the 1960s modernist home they ended up in offered both.

Andrea and Duncan are the first to admit that, from the outside, it's a bit of an ugly duckling. It's the oldest house on the block and hasn't seen a renovation since the early nineties. But they saw past what scared off most buyers (the falling-down shed in the yard, the pinky-beige kitchen laminate) and fell in love with its potential—its open floor plan and natural light. "Our vibe matched the house," she says. "We could already picture ourselves in it."

In just over a year, they've managed to turn the once-dated space into a cozy, eclectic hideaway, not through expensive renovations, but with savvy design choices that work with what's already there. The furniture, a mix of midcentury vintage finds and custom pieces by Duncan, accentuates the clean-lined architecture and retro aesthetic, while Andrea's modern artwork and super-bright textile collection add vivid bursts of color.

On the whole, they've taken a very minimal approach to decorating, preferring the laid-back feel of having a little over a lot. If anything, they've spent more time in the garden, where they've planted hibiscus bushes, a lemon tree, and lots of tomatoes, cucumbers, and pumpkins. Most afternoons you can find Andrea dragging a chair from one garden-view window to the next, chasing the sun across the yard and soaking in all her hard work.

MINI BUNGALOW

Heather Tierney
Venice, California

THERE ARE NO SUCH THINGS AS HALF MEASURES IN HEATHER
Tierney's world. She doesn't tiptoe lightly into big decisions.
Instead, she's more the go-full-tilt-and-see-what-happens type. So,
back in 2014, when The Butcher's Daughter founder decided to up
and move from Manhattan, where she'd been living for nearly a
decade, to Venice, she didn't just pack her boxes and call a moving
van. She shed her city-girl skin entirely and took a big gulp of the
California Kool-Aid.

She swapped her heels for sandals, cabs for a bicycle, and
her industrial Lower East Side loft for a tiny 1920s bungalow
located on one of Venice's charming canals. "I feel like I was
always meant to live here," says Heather. "Things just seem to
be falling into place for me." Those things include opening a
second location of her cult NYC juicery and café on Abbot
Kinney Boulevard, a few short blocks from her home, and
meeting a guy who likes to bring her breakfast in bed—toast
with jam and coffee—and take midnight canoe rides through
the canals.

The vibe Heather has so meticulously curated in her home
is quintessentially West Coast on every level—a little bit
seventies bohemian, a little bit beachy. She, admittedly, went a
tad wicker crazy, finally exploring a deep-seated fetish for
rattan furniture she'd been harboring for years. The bed
frames, the tables and chairs, even the bookshelves—all wicker.

ACROSS
It takes a certain kind
of person to see a
dilapidated shed and
think, "Hey, let's turn
it into a bathhouse."
But that's exactly how
this tiny outbuilding
became the dreamy
backyard escape you
see here.

ABOVE This curving wicker bed frame is one of the few non-vintage finds in the house. The goal is to one day coerce vines to grow up and over the top of the headboard. **ACROSS** Heather is a bit of a sleuth at upturning amazing rattan pieces. Her favorite source is Australia; she's been known to have entire containers of furniture shipped back to the States.

ABOVE This vintage Malm fireplace once sat in the backyard, but one winter in a house without heat was all it took for Heather to relocate it inside. **ACROSS** Function is in the eye of the buyer: Ask Heather what this is, for instance, and she'd say it's "a bar cart you can hang stuff on." Ask the folks at Venice Vintage Paradise, where she bought it, and they'd call it a coatrack.

"It's becoming a problem," she jokes. "Friends have threatened to hold an intervention if it starts feeling too *Golden Girls* around here."

But her penchant for indoor-outdoor furnishings is only half the picture. The fridge is stocked with fresh-pressed juices and organic wine from her shop. Every room smells of Sandoval's LOVE, a home spray that's a spicy blend of jasmine and neroli. Her record collection is a mix of old-school hip-hop and hippie icons. Macramé wall hangings mingle with vintage seashell planters. She converted the timber-clad shed out back into a bathhouse of sorts, with a daybed and large soaking tub. Even if part of you wants to tip up your nose at the picture-perfectness of it all, you can't help but want to live in the breezy, kicked-back world she's created, one that most certainly involves drifting around town on a beach cruiser.

As part of her Cali-girl metamorphosis, Heather has begun surfing or paddle boarding with her soon-to-be husband in the mornings. "I grew up in a landlocked state, so having water nearby is a luxury I never thought I'd have; like, is life allowed to be that good?" laughs Heather, who spent her childhood in Indianapolis. And though she fully concedes to being a terrible surfer, she still goes a few times a week and already purchased her first "real" board at Lone Wolfs surf shop for the day she's ready to graduate from the foam one she's been learning on. "It's just about being in the water for me. I could give a shit about being good or catching a huge wave. I just want to be out there trying."

ACROSS Palm trees are few and far between in the canals, so this one has become a symbol for the little bungalow. There's even a replica palm leaf etched into the glass door. **NEXT PAGE** In India, you'd use this vintage charpoy for sleeping, but line it with throw pillows and it becomes the ideal place to plop down with a book.

NORDIC A-FRAME

Mark Gibson and Maria McManus

Montauk, New York

WHEN YOU THINK OF MODERN ARCHITECTURE AND MONOCHROMATIC color palettes, warm and cozy aren't necessarily the first adjectives that come to mind—cold and stark, perhaps. But the weekend home of Mark Gibson and Maria McManus will forever change your mind about that. It flips those connotations on their heads, creating a space that's both efficiently streamlined and plop-down-anywhere comfortable.

The two purchased a 1980s A-frame in Ditch Plains (or "Ditch," as the locals call it) four years ago, after renting other homes in the area for over a decade. Mark is the restaurateur behind some of Manhattan's most loved watering holes, including The Wren and Wilfie & Nell. Maria runs the fashion merchandising and branding consultancy, PARISH. So this home was always meant to be a place for them to escape their crazy, planned-to-the-minute city lives—somewhere their two young daughters, Luella, five, and Poppy Rain, three, can run around like wildlings whenever they want.

It may be hard to picture, but this thoughtfully put-together home was once a sad, gray, pale blue–carpeted nightmare (think Palm Beach circa 1985, mirrored walls and all). The only thing it had going for it—aside from its surrounding population of fellow Irish expats—was its hop, skip, and jump proximity to the beach; a two-minute walk and you're there. Distance alone was enough to turn Mark and Maria from maybe-we'll-learn-to-surf-one-day people into enthusiastic, lesson-taking newbies.

ACROSS
The friendly (or some say, not-so-friendly) face greeting you in this entryway is a Druid mask by Irish ceramicist Louis Mulcahy; the family thinks of him as the wise man watching over the house.

It's sort of an unspoken rule at Ditch that surfing there requires at least one proper lesson with Steve, an instructor so notorious around those parts he goes by first name alone. Mark underwent that rite of passage a few summers back, and though, truth be told, he isn't sure how much he actually learned, the experience did help to inspire a surf vacation to The Harmony Hotel in Nosara, Costa Rica.

That particular slice of coast is known for its beginner-friendly breaks, and both Mark and Maria were surfing on their own after only a few lessons. "I was surprised how much I loved it," says Maria. "I actually *wanted* to surf every day." The trip ignited their interest in getting better. In fact, the first thing they bought when they got back to the States was a proper board from Air & Speed to keep at the house.

When Mark and Maria decided it was time to bring their tiny retreat into the twenty-first-century, they enlisted the help of

ACROSS Luella and Poppy Rain consider the front yard to be an extension of the beach, which is to say it's their own giant sandbox. So aside from the Dutch door being charming, it also allows direct views to the sand castle construction outside. **ABOVE** To seamlessly blend old and new, architect Thomas Ryan set off the wide cedar planks of the original home with thin vertical battens of the same wood (used across the additions), giving the angular structure a corduroy-like texture.

ABOVE Beachy this home is not. Maria bucked traditional East Coast design, and instead mixed natural accents (an Italian marble coffee table) with vintage finds (a Percival Lafer sofa), then overloaded the space with heaps of furry texture. **ACROSS** This couple can happily while away a Sunday in the kitchen, so counter space was always something they wanted in abundance, which is why, last minute, they added an island to complement the twelve-foot soapstone surface lining the back wall.

ABOVE This family loves a winter weekend in Montauk, when there's no one around but them and the crickets, and the only thing on the schedule is hunkering down in front of the wood-burning fireplace. **ACROSS** What to do in the tight corners, where the sloping ceiling meets the floor, was an ongoing discussion during construction. But the worry was for nothing, because the girls immediately saw it for what it was . . . a perfectly sized play nook.

architect Thomas Ryan. What started as a face-lift—like so many renovations do—turned into a taken-to-the-studs, eighteen-month rehab. For inspiration, they spent a lot of time looking at what Richard Meier was doing in Montauk in the sixties: "Small wood homes with very strong, geometric shapes, all painted one color," says Thomas, a Meier protégé himself. But rather than Meier's typical shade of choice, white, Maria wanted something that complemented the landscape and felt a bit Scandinavian, which is how they landed on the sooty, matte black exterior. "I love that it's oddly more subtle than other neutrals," says Maria. "It blends in with the trees around it."

It also feels less like a typical East Coast beach house, a deliberate stray from the norm that continues inside. Where the exterior is all sleek and moody, the interior couldn't be more sun-soaked and happy with a minimalist black, white, and gray design brought to life by layers and layers of wood and a playful twist on scale.

Whitewashed pine planks cover most of the walls. The floors are a mix of equally pale oak and concrete. Light fixtures are purposely off-kilter, whether it's the simplicity of the exposed bulb above the dining table or the dramatic size of the fixture in the sitting area. Vintage pieces—a leather sofa and dining chairs— mingle with cherished finds they've brought back from Ireland.

"It was a struggle because I wanted it done, but I didn't want to rush into buying something because I had to," says Maria. So the goal, post-renovation was to have a space that was just finished enough to function—which, for them, meant pulled-together enough to have friends and family over for cookouts. In fact, that's how they spent their first full summer in the new space. Mark played grill master on his new Big Green Egg, and surfed with buddies. Maria hosted yoga classes on the deck taught by a friend. They even christened an official house cocktail, a modified G&T: Hendrick's, equal parts tonic water and soda water, with a slice of lime and a slice of cucumber. Basically, summer in a glass.

Almost every room in this house opens
onto a deck, and the second-floor patio,
just off the kitchen, has become the place
where everyone congregates.

THE TACO MAKER

Tacos are the unofficial food of surfers, and in Rockaway Beach, New York, Andrew Field is the taco king. He's been slinging tortilla-wrapped goodness to the sand-covered masses for nearly a decade—first as a partner at Rockaway Taco, and now at his own joint, Tacoway Beach. He learned his craft in Mexico, where he spent five years running a restaurant south of Sayulita in the high season, and surfing and camping on the beach in the off-season. It was during the latter that he realized the inarguable genius of the taco as food. "When I'm surfing, the only thing that'll get me out of the water is hunger," he laughs, and in Mexico, that meant running up the beach, slapping a couple bucks down at a taco stand, shoving something delicious in his mouth, and then paddling back out. "It was this really simple, cheap thing."

That easy vibe was what he wanted to re-create in Rockaway and, fittingly enough, those first few summers, when he slept in a tent on the roof of the restaurant to make ends meet, it was the local surf community that rallied around him. It became *their* place, where local shapers like Joey Falcone met dawn patrol riders commuting from the city. These days, with the influx of beachgoers and new residents in the post-Hurricane Sandy revitalization, Tacoway Beach is a destination in itself with lines wrapping the building on summer weekends. So for 150 days straight, Andrew does nothing but make thousands of tacos, sneaking in the occasional surf session when he can. Then, come fall, he retreats to Mexico, where he does nothing but ride and reset for the next year . . . when the taco-making madness starts all over again.

Truck-a-Float is a joint project between Andrew, his girlfriend, Maribel Araujo, and two Venezuelan friends from Combo Collab. The floating pods are made from mostly recycled materials and used as extra sleeping quarters for guests.

HIDEAWAY IN THE HILLS

Desanka Fasiska

Los Angeles, California

"I'M A KOOK, I ADMIT IT." IT'S A HILARIOUSLY STRAIGHTFORWARD statement, no doubt. But anyone who's spent even a small amount of time with Desanka Fasiska will tell you that beating around the bush isn't really her thing. The ceramist-slash-designer—and newbie surfer—has a way of hop-skipping to the nut of a topic, whittling it down to its simplest (often bluntest) truth, especially when that topic happens to be her.

Ask her about her style, for instance, and she'll tell you it's "Biba goes to Big Sur" without missing a beat. (Think earth-goddess-meets-seventies glam.) Her backyard—with its winding paths, hidden hangouts, and funky aboveground pool—is her definition of "ballin' on a budget." The ceramics collection she makes for her lifestyle brand, Lux/Eros, is "totally fashion-centric," inspired by her years spent as a designer. And when it comes to the feeling she got the first time she laid eyes on the 1960s A-frame she calls home, well, that was all "nostalgic butterflies and pure, unadulterated love."

Desanka's infatuation with A-frames goes back to the one her father built as a vacation home on Cheat Lake in West Virginia, before she was even born. Her earliest days were spent water-skiing at that house, a memory that forever cemented the A-frame as the pinnacle of architectural excellence in her book. So when, as fate would have it, she happened across the same style house for sale in the Hollywood Hills within her budget, she essentially "lost her

ACROSS Jasper's favorite seat in the house is plopped down in front of the fireplace, which looks exactly as it did when the house was constructed. **ABOVE** What this sunny nook lacks in size, it more than makes up for in function: It's a guestroom, a mudroom, a laundry room, and a soon-to-be nursery.

ABOVE A boring bedroom door would have burst the amazing design bubble happening in this master suite. So instead, a beautifully carved room divider was turned into a hinged accordion door.
ACROSS Desanka wrapped a corner of the room in graphic cement tiles (by Grenada) to create what she calls "an open-concept en suite," equipped with a claw-foot tub.
PREVIOUS PAGE This living room sums up Desanka's thoughts on what every space needs to feel inviting: a little bit of wood mixed with an explosion of textures.

shit." It's important to understand that homes like this just don't exist anymore in the Hills; they've all been torn down to make room for soulless cement palaces, as Desanka likes to call the massive new constructions littering her neighborhood. So coming across this house that time forgot was essentially like finding the proverbial needle in a haystack.

"I was sold before ever seeing the inside," she says, which, it turns out, was a good thing because the inside was an industrial carpet–covered disaster. In the spirit of the original 1963 construction—and with her childhood dream home as a jumping-off point—Desanka set out to restore the home's original charm, refinishing the pine floors and shifting the footprint for better flow in the kitchen and second-floor master suite. But the goal was always to embrace the space's woodsy magic, so everything she brought into the house feels like a decadent nod to the outdoors: onyx and rose quartz countertops, handmade tiles, and lots of natural textiles mix with a sprinkling of retro glam moments that she lives for (brass hardware and light fixtures and a collection of Brutalist-inspired sculptures).

"If I could get away with never leaving my nest, I would," laughs Desanka, and, given her routine, it's not much of an exaggeration. Aside from the occasional road trip, she's figured out how to do most things from the comfort of "the lodge," a nickname given to her home by friends. Desanka entertains there, works there, and even holds workshops there, hosting classes on everything from macramé to mixing cocktails.

But there is one motivation that will always get her out the front door (other than an empty fridge), and that's surfing. She hasn't been at it long, a little over seven years, but she's been chasing the rush since getting her first taste in Santa Teresa, Costa Rica, in 2010. Come summer, she can be found most Fridays riding solo in Malibu. "I wear my kook status like a badge of honor," she jokes. "But in all seriousness, being out there is less about surfing for me, and more about the clarity that comes from just being on the water. Spacing out on my board keeps me hyper-focused in every other part of my life."

After years in the fashion industry, Desanka fell into the ceramics business by accident. While looking for an activity to help her get over a breakup, she joined a ceramics studio and ended up finding a new career. Though, considering her signature detail is a pyramid stud, it seems like her past is definitely influencing her future.

The end result of this kitchen renovation may be stunning, but Desanka took some knocks when she decided to tackle the task without a designer (like a materials snafu that left her without enough onyx to finish her countertops).

THIS PAGE AND ACROSS When she has the time (and she's not days away from having a baby), Desanka will make the hour-long drive to Venice, which has a beginner-friendly beach break that's more her speed.

DUNE-SIDE DECKHOUSE

David and Liz Netto
Amagansett, New York

SOME PEOPLE SURF TO BE IN NATURE, OTHERS SURF BECAUSE IT focuses the mind. Liz Netto surfs because it scares the shit out of her—and she likes that. "There's this moment when you're catching a wave, where you're on the edge of being terrified, and you just have to go for it," she says. That point, where fear tips in to sheer exhilaration, is what keeps Liz, a longboarder who's been riding for about eight years, going back for more.

The writer and documentary filmmaker, admittedly, found surfing later in life than most. It wasn't until two years after her daughter, Madelyn, who's now eleven, was born that she took her first official surf lessons in Sayulita, Mexico, while on a girls' trip. Ever since then, she's been enthusiastically making up for lost time. She's one of those fearless folks already in the water at Ditch Plains when the first dusty rays of sunshine break the horizon. "I love getting out there at 5 a.m., before almost everyone else," says Liz. "It's less crowded, and you catch more waves. But, it's also the best way to start your morning; by 8 a.m., I've already had the most amazing day."

Liz and her husband, David, a noted interior designer and writer, are both native New Yorkers who now split their time between Los Angeles and Amagansett. During the school year, they're in Silver Lake with Madelyn and Kate, David's oldest daughter, who's fifteen. But come summer (and whatever holidays and long weekends they can steal away), most of the

ACROSS
David would be the first to admit that he has a soft spot for books; he can't stop buying them. But the library here is a blink compared to the comprehensive collection at his home in Los Angeles.
NEXT PAGE
The master suite (which includes an in-room tub with direct sight lines to the sea) feels like you've climbed to the top of a lighthouse only to discover a decadent spa retreat.

ABOVE All the angular walls and built-in shelves leave little space for artwork, so the family room has become a pseudo gallery, showcasing favorite works. **ACROSS** "An incredible moment of theater" is how David describes the addition of an enormous window behind the fireplace, with its aquarium-worthy views of the dunes beyond.

ABOVE The slip of beach in front of the house just might be the last scrap of coast out east that, even at the height of summer, remains "uncrowded and scene free" as David likes to say.
ACROSS This family has an unspoken, though mutually followed, post-beach routine: outdoor shower, hot tub . . . always in that order.

family relocates to their happy little house on stilts mere steps from the Atlantic.

David purchased the home back in 2006 when he and Liz sold their apartment in Manhattan and officially moved to the West Coast. He wanted an excuse to keep spending his summers out east—something he's done all his life—and that excuse came in the form of the ugliest, cheapest house he could find on the water. "I fell in love with the spot but hated the house," says David of the beachfront property that abuts a nature preserve on one side. "Truly, there was nothing about this house that anybody could fall in love with."

That sentiment turned out to be not so true in the long run, though. Certain aspects of the house's quirkiness started to grow on him, mainly the sectional sophistication of its design. The floor plan is essentially a series of interlocking hexagonal rooms placed at various half levels (walking through it feels like winding your way up a lighthouse or conch shell). "Someone really thought about this," he says. "There's a kind of feng shui orientation between the house and how it relates to the dunes surrounding it and the ocean. But the aesthetic was terrible."

So David enlisted his architect friend Will Meyer, of Meyer Davis, to help him design something that kept the home's same

ABOVE It may sound counterintuitive, but Liz only surfs when she's on the East Coast. To "get her mojo back," she kicks off every summer by re-upping her skills with a few lessons from the guys at CoreysWave in Montauk. **ACROSS** This house sits on the narrowest stretch of Long Island, meaning it not only looks out over the ocean, it also has views of the bay and Napeague State Park in the distance.

footprint, roughly, while updating all the cheap, original, 1980s prefab materials. They added large casement windows, wrapped the exterior in cedar shingles, lined the interior walls with pale fir planks, blew out the top floor into one large master suite—all in a span of ten months, so they wouldn't miss a single summer season. "It has this sort of elegant identity now," he says. "Same shape, but better windows and finishes."

The goal was also to get away with needing as little furniture as possible. David put a lot of effort into designing built-ins; the bed frames, the night tables, the bookshelves are all permanent parts of the architecture. So the stand-alone pieces you do see are a mix of essentials (a sofa, a dining table) and personal objects—David's collection of eccentric vintage chairs, a lot of artwork, and even more books. The whole thing has an East Coast, beachy, bohemian vibe—but really, the vision was simply to make it a perfect surf hideaway for Liz.

CHASE

the
seekers

RETRO TRAILER

Greg Chait

Paradise Cove, Malibu

"HOW DID I *NOT* KNOW ABOUT THIS PLACE?" IS MOST PEOPLE'S response when they first lay eyes on Paradise Cove. And the answer to that question is actually simple: because the people who live there didn't want you to know about it.

Like most good things in the surf world, the magical retro trailer park that is Paradise Cove has been a closely guarded secret since the first residents—who were fishermen, not surfers—started parking their campers on the 85-acre beachfront lot back in the 1950s. It wasn't until the seventies that the local surf crews caught wind of the secluded neighborhood, with its proximity to Big and Little Dume Beach, and started moving in by the dozens. And that's when Paradise Cove permanently hit pause on allowing new settlements.

What you see today is essentially what residents laid out nearly fifty years ago: 265 trailers, practically stacked on top of one another, within walking distance of two of the best surf breaks in Malibu (though souped-up golf carts are the preferred mode of transport these days). A single cliff is all that separates the trailer park from its A-list neighbors and their $65 million–plus mansions.

Almost a decade ago, the cat was let out of the bag, so to speak, and Paradise Cove exploded into a super-cool place to be, luring in creative types like Greg Chait, founder of the lifestyle brand The Elder Statesman, who's been surfing on and off since

PREVIOUS PAGE
Malibu, California

ACROSS In this can't-spare-an-inch community, it's rare to have a patio that doesn't back up to another property. Greg's overlooks a small creek lined with trees that flows straight to the ocean.

ABOVE The pride and joy of this trailer—and the first thing you spot when you walk in the door—is Greg's sea blue General Electric fridge. **ACROSS** This custom sofa was built as much for function as it was for looks: deep enough for late-night party crashers to sleep on with a "pouf garage" underneath.

ABOVE Now that great waves are at his fingertips, Greg's relationship with surfing is far less obsessive than it once was. There's no more beating himself up if he can't paddle out for weeks at a time. **ACROSS** Greg's claims that this bed is "damn magical" to sleep on have been backed up by many a houseguest. It is almost perfect in its simplicity: no headboard, perched on the floor, and covered in soft blankets.

he was twelve. "Everyone who comes here wants to stay," says Greg, who bought his 1968 trailer three years ago. "Once I started visiting my friend Sofie Howard, who has a spot up the street, I knew I wanted to buy something here."

But even with the injection of all that new blood, Paradise Cove still remains somewhat charmingly frozen in time. There is an eclectic cast of characters—lifers and newbies, civil engineers and almond farmers, even a Sears washing machine repairman—all lured to this tiny subdivision where they can live a simple life by the water. "Everyone sort of respects the history of the place, the way of life around here," explains Greg. "Like even in my own trailer, I didn't want to redo too much. I like the vibe, so I left a lot of the stuff alone that would have scared the shit out of most people."

He's right; it's tough to tell where the original details end and Greg's renovations begin, which, of course, was the goal. He added a skylight in the main living area. He turned part of the covered outdoor patio into a room for his seven-year-old daughter, Dorothy. But he left eccentric details like a star-splattered tin ceiling and retro floral wallpaper alone, supporting his design decisions with the simple fact that "you couldn't re-create that look if you tried."

The things he brought into the space echo that same laid-back, less-is-more spirit. There's the stack of petrified wood slabs that he turned into a bedside table, and the collection of exotic poufs that are his version of dining chairs. His sofa is simply foam cushions covered in a patchwork of vintage fabric he picked up in Guatemala, which, incidentally, he also used in one of his menswear collections.

"When I'm out here, I'm surfing, I'm at the beach with Dorothy, I'm hanging out, having a good time. I'm not worrying about things that don't actually matter," says Greg. "We literally 'broke' the floor at one of my dance parties. There were forty people going insane in my living room, and now the trailer tilts a tiny bit. I didn't even care . . . hell, I was proud. *That's* how relaxed this place is."

Dylan Thomas: The legend and the poet

Leo & His Circle   Annie Cohen-Solal

LIVE/WORK LOFT

Shanan Campanaro and Nick Chacona
Williamsburg, Brooklyn

FIVE MINUTES IN SHANAN CAMPANARO AND NICK CHACONA's live/work loft and you'd think they were lifelong surfers. Even with three full-time employees in the 1,000-square-foot space, boards outnumber people two to one on most days—and that doesn't include the quiver they keep at Shanan's parents' home in San Diego or the ones in Nicaragua, where they're building a surf retreat. But, in truth, these two have only been seriously surfing for just over three years.

"I've always felt a strong connection to nature," says Shanan, whose eco-friendly home-goods collection, Eskayel, is known for its watery palettes and inkblot patterns. "The things I make and the things I have around my home are all meant to bring as much nature inside as possible." You see this in the chunks of sea glass sprinkled around the space, in the collections of shells splayed across bookshelves and the tops of dressers, and especially in the abstract seascapes that radiate from her line of wallpapers and fabrics. All in all, their city apartment feels more like an island oasis.

But Shanan, a self-proclaimed beach person, did not seriously consider the idea of surfing until she met Nick, now her husband and business partner. "When we met, Nick wasn't really into the beach. He's pink. He's pale. He sunburns," she jokes. But in 2008, on a trip to Montauk, New York, he completely surprised her by declaring his intention to start surfing. A year later, they took their

ACROSS
Most everything in this loft is either an Eskayel design or something the couple made to store Eskayel samples, like the large, framed tapestry rail.

NEXT PAGE
Surfing requires a certain amount of effort no matter where you live. But in a place like Brooklyn, that effort doubles—you're lugging gear to wherever you happened to park the night before, and you're drying wetsuits on a fire escape.

first lessons in Bali, which were followed by more trips and more lessons.

Surfing became the thing they did together when they traveled. "Even though we were terrible at it and looked like total spazzes in the water," she laughs, "we were at least equally terrible and equally spastic."

In 2013, the two got hitched in the Gili Islands, just off the coast of Lombok, Indonesia, where they spent as much time surfing as they did celebrating. "Something really clicked for us on that trip," she says. "It wasn't that we were all of a sudden good at surfing—we weren't and still aren't. But we realized that if we ever wanted to get better, we had to start surfing at home and not just on vacation."

So after they got back to the States they spent the entire summer of 2014 on the water. They bought their first boards—a 7'2" Gary Hanel Egg for her, a 7' Bruce Fowler Stoker for him—and rented a shack in Montauk. "The place was shit, but we were up and in the water by 5 a.m. every single day," she says. Over that three-month period, they got better—turning became easier, paddling out was not as exhausting. But what surprised Shanan more than their blossoming surf skills was their complete shift in lifestyle. "All of a sudden, I was a morning person," she says. "We were both eating healthier, going out less. It felt amazing."

Since then, surfing—and all the life changes it inspired—has been an important part of the couple's day-to-day life. At least three times a week they are out at Gilgo Beach in Long Island before work, though Shanan admits to being a total wimp about getting in the water when the temp outside drops below freezing. But nine to ten months out of the year, they have a morning routine that's pretty much set in stone: Get up at five. Be in the water by seven. Surf two to three hours. Be home and working by eleven. "It sounds exhausting," she says, "but I'm actually so completely awake after I start my day in the water. Surfing is better than coffee, I swear."

ABOVE No matter the time of year, this serene bedroom—with its textural layers and beachy accents—always feels like summer. **NEXT PAGE** What started as a one-third to two-thirds work/life split in regards to space is reversed these days, forcing the couple to be fluid with their floor plan, which often has to be changed up daily.

HILLTOP HACIENDA

Brittney Borjeson
Sayulita, Mexico

IT TAKES A CERTAIN KIND OF PERSON TO TRADE IN A SUCCESSFUL, hyper-focused life in New York City for a fly-by-the-seat-of-your-pants existence in Sayulita, Mexico. But for Brittney Borjeson that decision all boiled down to one simple realization: she would rather be living a life she loves every single day than living for the dream of a future that may or may not come to fruition.

"I think I was a low level of miserable my whole life and just didn't know it," says Brittney. "Then I took a trip to Sayulita in 2010, and I felt good, really good, like better-than-a-vacation-should-feel good." So she spent the next year and a half chasing that vacation high, traveling back and forth to Mexico, trying to figure out how to make a life there. What she came up with was a small business plan that tapped in to the very thing in Sayulita that she fell in love with in the first place—its people.

Evoke The Spirit is a workshop-slash-boutique that carries traditionally crafted Mexican wares, many of them designed by Brittney, all of them made by local artisans. "The level of quality artisanship here, especially among the Wixáritari people, is amazing," says Brittney. "Everything is done the old way, the way it's been done for generations." This means that most of what you find in her shop—yarn-painted skulls, macramé wall hangings, and ceramics—has only ever been touched by the hands of the artist who made it. Take the graphic wool rugs she carries, for instance. Creating one is not simply a matter of her bringing the

ACROSS
Brittney's bedroom opens out onto what she calls "the downstairs garden," a semi-shaded landing that's home to her favorite place to spend an afternoon . . . her hammock.

NEXT PAGE
Brittney is a devoted rider of DANC surfboards by Dan Cobley. All three of her boards were shaped by him with her specific surfing goals in mind.

ABOVE The kitchen island doubles as a breakfast bar and countertop, and is simply a slab of raw wood that's been rubbed down with coconut oil. **ACROSS** As soon as she moved in, Brittany covered every surface in a fresh coat of white paint, something she repeats yearly to keep things feeling crisp.

Finding new uses for leftover materials is one of Brittney's superpowers. The wooden platform beneath her cactus garden, for instance, is one end of the slab of wood that was used to make her coffee table.

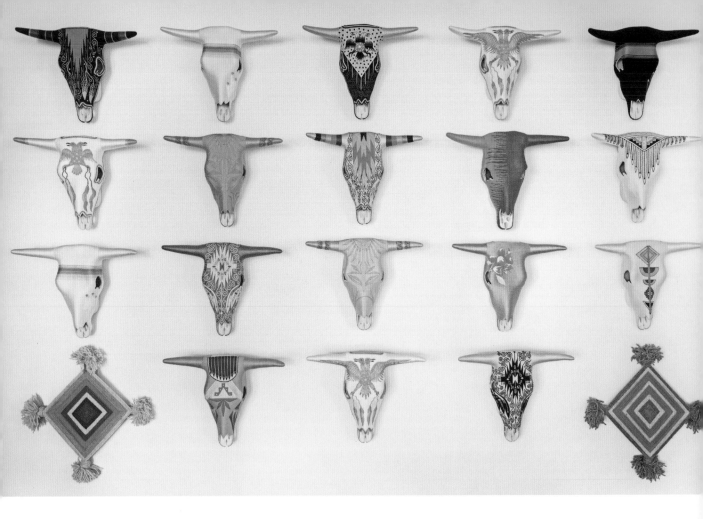

ABOVE It takes an artisan days to make a single one of these stunning skulls. The ancient (and sacred) technique is called yarn painting, and it involves coating a skull in beeswax before methodically tapping yarn into the wet surface to create graphic patterns.
ACROSS Above the guestroom bed hangs an *Ojo de Dios* (or God's Eye), which is traditionally given as protection to newborns and is also a symbol for welcoming new members into a tribe.

design to a local weaver. That weaver also makes the materials needed to create that rug, spinning piles of sheered wool into yarn, and hand-dyeing the yarn using dried vegetables or leaves and a paste created from crushed bugs. "It's amazing to watch something transform from a part of the earth into something really beautiful that you can put in your home."

Finding this level of meaningfulness in her work and loving the people she interacts with on a daily basis were all part of Brittney's vision for living a more beautiful life—as was making time to surf, something she has no remorse about saying is the center of her world. "Being completely synchronized with an extremely unstable event, a wave, is the most incredible feeling in the world," she says. "I will blow off everything for that feeling." And that's no exaggeration; if there's a good swell, she will ignore dinners, work appointments, even birthday parties.

Proximity to her favorite break, Punta Burros, is one of the reasons she chose the tiny hilltop hacienda she lives in. It's a ten-

ABOVE The master bedroom is lined in soft linen curtains, which diffuse light and make the whole space feel as if you're cocooned in a cloud.
ACROSS Brittney believes painting or lacquering wood is a crime. Over time, these dining chairs will turn a pretty shade of gray, and she's looking forward to watching that natural evolution occur.

Part of the charm in Brittney's make-no-plans approach to living is that simple moments—like stopping for a beer with your boyfriend—can turn into magical moments, and there's no I-should-be-doing-something-else guilt involved.

minute drive to that beach, two blocks from her shop, and has sweeping views of the Pacific. From the outside, it's an absolute paradise. Inside, however, is a different story. Like most traditional Spanish homes in the area, this one, at its core, can feel pretty sterile. It's all cement walls, tile floors, and built-in furnishings. So everything Brittney brought into the house, most of which is from her shop, was meant to add warmth and a sense of homeyness. Layers of wool rugs, reed mats, and colorful cushions mix with live-edge wood tables and collections of things she's found in nature (groups of feathers or dried grass). She likes to joke that in New York her furniture would have been refined, polished, and perfect. But here, it's made with an ax and a chainsaw.

Living in a jungle in Mexico, even in a house as dreamy as the one Brittney's created, isn't without its own set of unique obstacles, though. Sweeping rivers of water out the front door is a reality during tropical storm season. Running outside to the boiler mid-shower to check the pilot light is also a regular occurrence. And don't even get her started on the topic of grounded electricity, of which there is none. (She had to build a wooden box around her fridge to keep it from shocking her at the slightest bump.) But along with her planned-to-the-minute life in New York, Brittney has also given up traditional ideas of perfection, because perfect for her is a house full of idiosyncrasies and a happy life with the ocean firmly at the heart of it.

BROOKLYN BROWNSTONE

Julia Chaplin
Carroll Gardens, Brooklyn

EVERYBODY SHOULD BE LUCKY ENOUGH TO HAVE A SURF GURU, especially one as epic as Garth Murphy. Where an actual surf instructor will teach you only things like pop-ups and duck dives, Garth, a local legend in the Baja surf scene and the man who taught Gypset creator Julia Chaplin to ride nearly two decades ago, started with what truly matters: how to *not* look like an idiot with a surfboard. (Rule number one: Never, ever walk on the beach with a leash around your ankle, which basically signals to everyone that you're a newbie.)

Garth, who was part of the whole surf scene that Tom Wolfe wrote about in *The Pump House Gang,* is far more concerned with riding style than technique—which may sound like one and the same, but style, how you look on your board in the water, is a concept that a lot of lifelong surfers argue is lost on the newest generation of swell seekers. "Garth used to say, 'You can stand up on a wave, but what's your body doing? Are your shoulders slumped? Do you look like a gorilla on a surfboard?'" says Julia. "And he's right. Look at the big historic riders; they all have great style. Guys like Gerry Lopez, who crouches down low, or Miki Dora, who has this lazy lean." Julia's signature style, incidentally, falls somewhere between the two: Straight back. Bent knees. Great wetsuit.

Julia grew up with hippie parents who moved every few years to a different end-of-the-road locale—places like Key West, the

ACROSS

When Julia bought this nineteenth-century brownstone two years ago, a lot of the original architecture was completely unsalvageable. So she brought in an expert to replicate the single surviving bit of molding around the rest of the space.

CHASE

100

ACROSS Julia has particular (often expensive) taste in furniture. But she'd rather have nothing than the wrong thing, which is why she spent a year hunting for this Angelo Mangiarotti dining table. **ABOVE** As much as she loves a hippie influence, Julia also has a soft spot for the occasional hit of bling, a fetish that comes from frequenting NYC hot spots like Mr. Chow with her dad in the eighties.

BROOKLYN BROWNSTONE

103

ABOVE Wall-to-wall carpeting and the built-in platform bed was inspired by famed designer/architect Paul Rudolph, who used the same treatment in Halston's iconic New York home back in the sixties. ACROSS Despite having a bedroom to herself, Tuesday has been "living" almost exclusively in her Aztec tent, which she's set up like her very own mini-house of sorts.

Bahamas, and Todos Santos in Mexico, where her father still has a house today. And though she happily inherited their gypsy spirit—she'll spend weeks on the West Coast, a month in Mexico, travel to barely charted coasts in Indonesia, all on a whim—she never thought she'd get into surfing. "I remember as a kid watching my dad surf, and he would just get killed out there, like totally gnarly wipeouts," she says. "It looked dangerous and scary and I thought there was no way that I would ever do that."

But all that changed the day Garth approached her on the beach in Todos Santos when she was in her mid-twenties and asked if she wanted to learn. In that moment, when she said yes only because she was bored, her life was transformed. "The whole surf vibe inspires everything I do now," says Julia. If she hadn't learned to surf, she never would have come up with the idea for *Gypset,* her bestselling book series that has spiraled into a popular brand with its own boho-inspired clothing collection.

In many ways, the Brooklyn brownstone Julia shares with her six-year-old daughter, Tuesday Miller, is the embodiment of that vibe as well—not in a beachy way, but in the sense that it's beautifully pared down; it "travels light," as the surf mantra goes. Her whole vision for the nineteenth-century home was a broken-down palace; the idea the Rolling Stones had when they recorded *Exile on Main St.* in the seventies in the South of France, where they notoriously rented a villa, pushed all the furnishings to the side, and lived on the floor.

So the furniture in Julia's home, what little of it she has, all sits low to the ground and is surrounded by lots of blankets, throw pillows, and vintage rugs. Her bed is simply a mattress perched atop a carpeted platform. Her living room is essentially made up of only three pieces: an Art Deco Chinese rug from the 1920s that she inherited from her grandfather, a giant mirror she found at a salvage yard, and a hard-sought Mario Bellini leather sofa system from the seventies, which she bought for two reasons—all the pieces move and it's impossible to sit on it in a formal way.

"I'm promoting a horizontal lifestyle—but not in the way you're thinking," laughs Julia. "It's how true nomads live—a lot of rugs and textiles, no furniture. Home is wherever you happen to land." Even better if that landing is a soft one.

The one item Julia doesn't give a second thought about stockpiling is exotic textiles, which she's brought home as souvenirs for years: Berber blankets, suzanis, Beni Ourain rugs, Mexican quilts, etc. The collection is constantly shuffled from room to room—and occasionally carried to the backyard for mother-daughter snugglefests.

THE ECO-MINDED DESIGNER

When former longboarding pro Kassia Meador came up, part of the thrill of being out on the water was the wildlife she encountered. With the sad state of today's oceans (and a lot of beaches, in general), surfers are far more likely to spot a school of plastic bags than Garivaldi fish—and that's something Kassia is trying to change. Apart from her noble habit of picking up trash she comes across on the beach (something, she reminds, everyone can do), her surf label called Kassia is making major strides in countering the environmental effects of bringing beautiful, high-quality pieces (wetsuits, swimsuits, incredible-smelling surf wax, etc.) into the world.

She's making the biggest difference by putting smart production practices into action. "Nothing gets thrown away or wasted," she explains. "The large pieces left over from cutting our wetsuits are made into swimsuits or leggings, what's left after that becomes tote bags, and any scraps too small to sew into something else become part of our wetsuit recycling program." The recycling program is probably her biggest and most promising initiative. It incentivizes folks to send Kassia their used wetsuits (from any brand) to be turned into other lifestyle products. "For a lot of people the cost of creating, of producing things en masse, is sort of out of sight, out of mind. But when you're a surfer and it's in your sight all the time, it's not so easy to ignore."

If the waves are working at Malibu First Point, that's where you'll find Kassia. It's been her go-to since she first picked up a board, back when she only wanted two things: to ride with her dad and make her *Gidget* dreams reality.

CONTEMPORARY BARN

Blake and Heather Mycoskie

Topanga Canyon, California

BLAKE AND HEATHER MYCOSKIE'S INTRODUCTION TO SURFING, years before they'd even met, couldn't have been more clashingly different. Blake's first time out involved getting tossed around by the waves and yelled at by the locals in San Diego, while Heather learned to ride from her friend, Red Hot Chili Peppers' Anthony Kiedis, on a private beach in Malibu. As opposite as their experiences were, they each came away with a bad case of the surfing bug that, years later, on the other side of the country, would lead to one awe-inducing meet-cute.

At the time of her West Coast trip, Heather was living in New York, working as a model for FORD. So when she got home, she went into surf-search mode. That's when her dad, a surfer back in his heyday, directed her to Montauk—or, as he called it, "the end-end-end-end-end of Long Island." She snagged a job at the local surf shop Air & Speed, lived in the apartment above, and spent the summer cruising.

Blake, the founder of TOMS, on the other hand, a little rocked by his initial experiences in the water, didn't get serious about surfing until 2009, when the search for a quiet spot to work on his first book, while also doing something active, landed him in Witch's Rock, Costa Rica. He dedicated a month to writing and taking surf lessons with an instructor, which is what finally got him hooked on riding. So when it came time to wrap up his manuscript almost a full year later, he decided to keep the

ACROSS

Heather brought a lot of influences from her New York days into this entryway. The stained glass is by Brooklyn artist Colin Adrian, and the floors are repurposed wood from the Coney Island boardwalk, where her grandparents met when they were fifteen.

CHASE

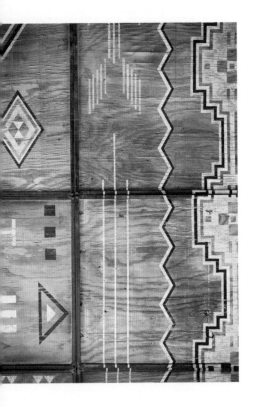

write-surf rhythm alive, and headed to Montauk, where, on the hunt for surf wax one day, he stumbled into Air & Speed and met Heather for the very first time.

Seven years, one wedding, and an adorable baby boy later, these two are still big wave lovers—though Heather, admittedly, is more of a fair-weather surfer, saving her board time for the couple's frequent trips to warmer waters. But Blake has become a year-round rider, heading out for dawn patrol a few times a week to hit Topanga or Sunset before his two-year-old son, Summit, gets up. Surf trips to the Maldives with a crew of eight of his best friends are a yearly outing. And all of their warm-weather vacations have turned into surf vacations to Hawaii, Mexico, and Fiji. "It's a huge part of my life now, and I hope it will be part of our kid's life," says Blake. "That's one of the things that brought us to Topanga Canyon, seeing all the dads and moms with their kids out on the local breaks. I wanted that."

They moved to Topanga in 2014, after more than two years of looking for the right property. That amount of house hunting may sound excessive, but a cookie-cutter home was never in the cards for these two. They have a thing for personal spaces with a touch of whimsy, like the sailboat they lived on for years or the teepee they got married in. "When we first met, I talked about building a tree house in Topanga. It felt like the logical next step after the boat," says Blake. It was that vision that drew them to this 1970s kit house, nestled at the tip-top of a gently sloping property sprinkled with stately oaks and a winding creek bed. "The rooms, most of them anyways, are at canopy-level, so I feel like I'm in a tree house, especially in my office."

With the help of Los Angeles–based design studio Hammer and Spear, Blake and Heather embarked on a yearlong, tip-to-toe renovation, a project they approached with a mindfulness and

ABOVE The idea of incorporating an Aztec-inspired hand-painted ceiling in the downstairs den was something Blake had seen and fallen in love with years before—and something he was adamant about incorporating into the house. **ACROSS** Heather found out she was pregnant in the middle of their renovation. Aside from significantly shortening their initial deadline, the design team had to scramble to create this incredibly cozy, Noah's Ark–themed nursery. **NEXT PAGE** Board envy is not something this couple suffers from. Though extremely edited, their quiver includes exactly what they need and nothing more.

ACROSS Tucked away in a corner of the downstairs family room, this industrial table is *the* spot for game nights with friends. **ABOVE** The color palette in Heather's office—which is really part lounge space, part workspace—is a more feminine spin on the earthy reds and browns you see in the rest of the house.

attention to detail that have become the calling cards of their lifestyle. Instead of big vendors, they brought in artists like Patch PSS Design Cult to build incredible feats of custom woodwork and Mark James Yamamoto to hand-paint a graphic ceiling in the den. In lieu of new furnishings, they used antiques. Their collection of vintage rugs, for instance, were layered, one on top of another, in almost every room—a nod to the lobby of the Bowery Hotel, their favorite place to stay in Manhattan.

But what makes this house feel most like home to Blake and Heather are the inventive ways the couple's cherished—and often mammoth-size—personal treasures (a set of Indian doors, a Balinese desk, a one-story Buddha statue, even the teepee they were married in) were worked in to the rustic, comfortable design. "We've been collecting these pieces for years, but we have never actually lived with them," says Heather. "So when we finally moved in, being surrounded by all of these things that tell our story made the house feel as if we'd already been there forever." For a couple that prioritizes meaningfulness above all else, that feeling, and the thoughtfulness with which this refuge in the trees was created, is the ultimate tribute to the lives they want to lead.

ABOVE With a two-year-old in the house, finding a peaceful space to meditate isn't as simple as closing the bedroom door, so the teepee has become Blake's de facto quiet place.
ACROSS Slide these custom couches together and they make a queen-size bed for overnight guests and, eventually, Blake is guessing, little kid slumber parties.

CONVERTED B&B

Yves Béhar and Sabrina Buell
West Marin, California

ACROSS

In its past life as a bed and breakfast, more than three hundred couples got hitched here. Occasionally, people stop by to visit the sight of their nuptials, a request Yves and Sabrina accommodate (often over a shared bottle of wine).

NEXT PAGE

This 32-foot-long outdoor picnic table is made from a single piece of salvaged redwood that was pulled out of a burnt forest.

THERE'S AN OLD ADAGE THAT SAYS THE BEST SURFER OUT THERE IS the one having the most fun. That idea gets at the heart of how Yves Béhar and Sabrina Buell feel about riding. Because if there's one thing they've learned from over a decade of surfing in NoCal it's this: you can have an incredible time on a shitty day.

For Yves, founder of Fuseproject and the man behind all of Jawbone's sleek designs, that realization went hand in hand with setting aside some of his preconceived notions on perfection. "I think that in our modern lives, there is the expectation that everything has to be perfect," he says. "But you can't just step on a surfboard and expect that the elements are going to be there for you, that they're going to be perfect."

In other words, you can't make the waves better, so it's your job to take advantage of whatever comes your way—a philosophy that Sabrina, a partner at the art advisory firm Zlot Buell + Associates, shares. "It's funny, everybody calls me the 'honey badger' because I will go for any wave—like aggressively, like I'm not picky at all," she laughs. "I'd rather take twenty waves that aren't good, than sit and wait for one that's perfect."

Back before they became a family of six (they have three kids together, Sylver, five, Soleyl, two, and Saylor, almost one, and Yves has a nine-year-old son, Sky), they were just surfing buddies. "We met at a party at my dad's house, and Yves asked if I wanted to go surfing. I called my brother and was like, 'You have to teach me

PREVIOUS PAGE A former owner built this crazy-cool indoor pool that also feels like a greenhouse. It's surrounded by night-blooming jasmine, so the whole space smells as magical as it looks. **ABOVE LEFT** This door, decked out in stars, leads to the master closet, which has doubled as a cozy (temporary) nursery for all their little ones. After the first year, they move to the kids' bunkroom with the rest of the gang.

ABOVE Yves and Sabrina prefer wide-open spaces to a room that's overly furnished, so there's a lot of extra built-in seating around the house, like this cushioned bench in the master suite with direct views of the garden.

ACROSS The couple's interest in art, surfing, and 1970s design converge in the living room where pieces from a Mario Bellini sectional sofa (which get moved around as needed) mix with a Robert Longo Wave print, a gift from Sabrina to Yves. **ABOVE** There's never a clear idea of how many to expect for dinner, so a good portion of the weekend is spent in the kitchen, cooking up easy dishes like grilled salmon snagged from the local fishing docks.

how to surf right now,' and so he did," laughs Sabrina. "That's how we got to know each other . . . in the water." And it's still a core part of who they are as a couple more than a decade later. They surf together year-round. They got engaged in the water on a trip to Indonesia. Their idea of date night is a surf outing—minus the kids, minus the phones.

Surfing is so ingrained in their lives that they keep a family compound in the coastal haven of West Marin, just an hour north of their apartment in San Francisco. The cliff-top home has had many lives. It was hand-built back in the seventies by the original owner, who kept chickens, horses, and pigs on-site (as one was apt to do in California at that time), and also moonlighted as a bed-and-breakfast for a flash in the early 2000s. So aside from the main structure, an art-filled, low-key, "wannabe East Coast beach house," there are lots of little outbuildings on the property—an aviary, an indoor pool, and a handful of guest cabins.

That extra sleeping space comes in handy given Yves and Sabrina's fast-and-loose interpretation of an open-door policy. Yves will invite friends. Sabrina will invite other friends. And it's anyone's guess who—or how many—will show up. It's the reason their outdoor dining table seats forty, and why their separate kitchen, dining, and living rooms were opened up to make one big space for entertaining. The vibe is casual, with people milling about inside and out, and the house is designed with that in mind. There are plenty of cozy seating arrangements and just as many nooks to sneak off to for a quiet moment alone.

On any given weekend, there's usually an oddball mix of surfers and artists, curators and friends over from Europe—you might even find Alice Waters in the kitchen. "It's very informal. People show up on their own time," says Yves. "It happens quite often that we'll go for a surf and come home to people just sitting on the deck hanging out, waiting for us."

ACROSS The couple's quiver falls into one of two categories: those shaped by friends (they've had five made at Puka Puka in Hawaii) and those shaped by old-school names like Dick Brewer, Randy Cone, and Gerry Lopez.

CARVE

the
riders

COASTAL CABIN

Simon Taylor and Kirsty Davey

Jan Juc, Australia

DIVING INTO A TUBE, BEING COMPLETELY COCOONED IN WATER, IS one of those spiritual, connected-to-nature moments that only surfers truly understand. If you haven't done it, you want to. If you have, it's what keeps you paddling out for more. Most folks say the experience is indescribable, but Simon Taylor, a Bells Beach local, does a pretty good job of cutting to the heart of it. "There is this amazing thing that happens with sound when you're inside a wave," says Simon. "All the noise goes away, and there is just this quiet 'wom, wom, wom' in your ears. It's like you found a special place that's all yours, and then you shoot out the other end."

Simon picked up his first board when he was ten. As far as vices go, surfing certainly isn't a baddie (as the Aussies would say). But that *is* the type of relationship Simon says he has with riding. It's not a hobby. It's not a thing he simply enjoys. It's something he can't live without, something that keeps him functioning at normal, so to speak. "If I haven't been for a week," says Simon, "I don't feel quite myself. I get antsy." His wife, Kirsty Davey, would nod her head in agreement with that assessment. "I can always tell when he needs a surf. Sometimes I'll just point and say, 'Go get in the ocean.'"

When Kirsty and Simon first met, back in 2007, they were both living in Melbourne. Kirsty was working at Lonely Planet and Simon had just started his business, Monster Jam Agency, where he reps indie skate and surf brands, like Chilli and Lost

ABOVE Both Simon and Kirsty work from home, so they each have tiny "office" nooks. Simon's garden-view retreat is tucked away in what used to be a laundry room. **ACROSS** This mostly original, always reliable chariot (known to family and friends as Penny Lane) is Kirsty's first baby. She picked up the 1965 Falcon Coupe back in 2008 after dreaming of owning one since she was a teen.

Surfboards. Practically every Friday, Saturday, and Sunday were
spent making the three-hour round trip to the Surf Coast and
back. That was when they figured out they were doing things all
tangled up and backward. "It made more sense for us to live where
the surf was and figure out how to make Melbourne the place we
go for work," says Simon, though, in his case, it helps that Jan Juc,
the tiny coastal hamlet they landed in, is smack in the middle of
Australia's surf industry; Rip Curl and Quicksilver ("Quickie" to
the locals) are both headquartered one town over in Torquay. That
was eight years ago. Kirsty has since opened an online shop called
Otis & Otto, and they haven't looked back once.

The house they rent is the first and only house they looked at,
and one of the oldest in Jan Juc. "There are a lot of local myths and
legends about our place," says Kirsty, who heard from one of the
previous owners that the original structure was built at the turn of
the last century in Ballarat, a city roughly sixty miles inland, and
hauled to the coast in the 1950s. "It's had many lives and was a
vacation rental for years before we moved in."

That, to an extent, helps explain some of its many
eccentricities: the fact that rooms appear to have been added at
random over the decades, so there's an odd mix of fifties, sixties,
and seventies architecture. Or the fact that despite being a beach
house, its walls and ceilings are clad in Baltic pine, making it feel
more like a cozy cabin that belongs in the woods. It does, however,
leave the greatest design mystery of all unsolved—the case of the
crazy carpets. "Nobody seems to know where they come from,"
says Kirsty with an eye roll. Almost every room features a different
color or pattern, the main attraction being the master bedroom,
which is decked out in an uber-bright tropical print.

"We know, the house is kooky . . . but we love that about
it," says Kirsty. "Even the carpet has grown on me at this point."
Despite getting finger wags from friends about spending money
on a rental, Simon and Kirsty have undertaken a few updates over
the years to smooth out the rough edges, and make it feel more
like a family home for their five-year-old daughter, Mali, including
painting some of the walls and ceilings white to brighten things
up a bit. But, for the most part, they've let things be. Staying
in a long-term rental has helped them to lead not minimal but

Vladimir Tretchikoff's 1952
painting *Chinese Girl* is as
much a symbol of midcentury
design as an Eames chair
(though not nearly as well
known today). After coveting
his work for years, Kirsty
received this print as a gift.

uncomplicated lives. "We live with less," she says, "but we love what
we have."

The one exception to that philosophy might be Simon's
surfboard collection, which is loved but by no means small. There's
usually anywhere between twenty-five and thirty boards in his
quiver, depending on the season. He has a few guns and semi-guns
by Chilli that he surfs a lot, also a handful of boards by Wayne
Lynch that he enjoys almost as much as the stories surrounding the
local surf legend. (There's the one about Lynch and his buddies
wreaking havoc on the first paved road into Bells Beach, or the

time he dodged going to the Vietnam War by refusing to leave the
water when draft officers tracked him down.)

Everything is organized in a shed-turned–man cave out back.
Vintage boards are stowed in the rafters; the rest of the quiver is
sorted along the walls, largest to smallest, according to the size
wave they work for. "I move things in and out a lot; the shortboards
I change up probably every six months," says Simon. "I think, as a
surfer, I have this never-ending need to search for the perfect
board; it's like the same need to hunt for the perfect wave."

Simon's most prized (but not
too prized to ride) vintage board
collection includes a 6'2" Hot
Buttered Single Fin by Terry
Fitzgerald (an iconic Aussie
shaper from the seventies),
and a 6'0" Hot Stuff Single Fin
by the late Al Byrne.

ABOVE Houseguests are a reality when you live on the coast. In the summer they come for the sun, in the winter for the swells. So this guest room sees a lot of action. **ACROSS** Kirsty's collection, now Mali's, of Dean & Son books—a nineteenth-century British publisher known for its imprints of classic children's stories—started with her dad's copy of *Twenty Thousand Leagues Under the Sea.*

DESERT HOMESTEAD

Channon and Bianca Roe

Ojai, California

THE PERFECT WAVE; IT'S THE EQUIVALENT OF THE ELUSIVE Sasquatch to surfers. Tales of its existence are told as lore around bonfires. But die-hard riders, like actor-slash–interior designer Channon Roe, will chase these mythical swells to the ends of the earth and back, come hail or high water. He has dropped in on some of the best breaks in the world, from Hawaii's North Shore to Raglan in New Zealand, one of the longest left point breaks around (and every goofy-footed boarder's dream). But unfortunately for him—or rather, unfortunately for his lovely wife, Bianca—one of his most epic rides, his first at Australia's Byron Bay, did, in fact, involve hail and high water . . . and frogs (yes, frogs).

The story goes like this: It was Channon's first trip to Australia with Bianca, who is originally from Melbourne, and it was Christmas. After making the family-and-friends rounds, they hopped in a tiny rental car, strapped three surfboards to the roof, and started the eight-hour trek from Sydney to Byron Bay with Bianca driving. The two were so excited they didn't notice the rain as it turned to hail, or the miles of stopped traffic heading the opposite direction. It wasn't until it literally started raining frogs (a phenomenon that, as it turns out, does happen in Australia) that they pulled into a small beach town and realized they were driving directly into a cyclone. After hunkering down for the night, they finally made it to their destination the next day, and, much to

ABOVE "They don't make 'em like they used to" is the perfect mantra for this couple's collection of beautifully lived-in vintage furniture, like these Italian chairs from the seventies. **ACROSS** Their travels abroad always end with the same question: how are we going to get this home? They lugged the set of eighteenth-century Basque church stools back from Biarritz, France.

This Chris Christenson C-bucket (a birthday surprise from Bianca) was the missing link in Channon's quiver, "the perfect shape," he says, "for guys who grew up on a shortboard, but are now looking for a more soulful cruising experience."

Channon's complete surprise, the place was empty. "I was out there almost by myself, and it was everything I wanted it to be," he says. "Mother Nature can really make you work for the good ones."

Channon has been in the water since before he could walk. He's the product of a long line of riders and grew up during the heyday of Orange County's surf scene in the mid-seventies to early eighties. (He's even named after one of his dad's favorite local shapers, Channin Surfboards.) Any surf historian will tell you that this pocket of the coastline at that time—Corona Del Mar, San Clemente, Newport Beach, Laguna—was a melting pot of beach culture and a burgeoning lifestyle scene. It was a moment, just like London in the sixties was a moment. "You had these die-hard surfers, who were basically rock stars, rolling up to the beach in fur coats and Porsches," says Channon. "Then there were the artists and the shapers, the drug dealers and the swingers, the architects and musicians; it was a wild time and definitely left a lasting impression."

ACROSS There are too many perfectly imperfect moments to count in this house, like the bedside vignette in the guestroom, which includes a wall hanging by Edith Zimmer.
ABOVE LEFT The driftwood sculpture is by a local artist who scours the beach for "treasures" and then turns them into art.
ABOVE A Native American Indian profile, by Ojai artist Lana Rasmussen, hangs just outside the master suite.

ABOVE When Channon says he is crazy about textiles, he's not exaggerating. He snaps up everything from twentieth century Japanese boro fabrics to Navajo rugs dating back to the 1800s. **ACROSS** Funny thing about the surf world . . . bartering is still an acceptable purchasing practice. Channon traded a vintage surfboard for this 1960s oil painting that Bianca spotted and fell in love with.

ABOVE Never one to shy away from a hug, Marlon's most common (and so incredibly adorable) post-nap request is "can we snuggle, just for a minute?"
ABOVE RIGHT The first veggie patch has been planted alongside the house with a row of citrus trees in the works. By next season, this couple is hoping these bowls of fruit will be from their own yard.
ACROSS Channon has been channeling his inner Francis Mallmann (an Argentinian chef known for his wild, open-fire cooking methods), grilling up fresh ingredients right in his own backyard.

It was this creative, outdoorsy, vagabond spirit that Channon and Bianca were after when, six years ago, they transitioned their second home in the hippie hideaway of Ojai into their primary one. "Moving was about getting back to the California I grew up in," says Channon. But, in truth, it was also about giving his son, Marlon, a childhood similar to his own. Ojai is known for its roots-y surf community. Rincon, arguably one of the top five point breaks in the world, is thirty minutes away. So for Channon, it feels like Laguna in the eighties—"minus the flash . . . and the drugs."

What Channon and Bianca have created in Ojai, though, is not just a home; it's more a mini–bohemian universe of sorts. They have a 1976 Airstream permanently parked in their front yard, which is part mad-scientist man cave (where Channon tinkers away on his latest interior design projects) and part guest quarters. There's a teepee behind their midcentury ranch house. And then there's the shop, In the Field, a lifestyle store the couple opened in 2014 that carries goods from local makers and friends, as well as treasures they've picked up on their travels.

ABOVE Technically, Channon's twenty-five or so boards live in the garage, but more often than not they're spread out in the house, the yard, the back of the truck—basically, everywhere.

ABOVE RIGHT The framed *Dogtown and Z-Boys* poster in Marlon's room was passed down from Dad. It's signed by director Stacy Peralta and was given to Channon at a premiere for the cult skate documentary.

ACROSS Marlon is reaching the age where he wants to surf with Dad, which for now translates to riding doubles on a boogie board.

NEXT PAGE Something brand new doesn't stand a chance around here, which is why this couple gravitates toward furniture that, as they say, already has a good patina on it.

Life in this hippie utopia is a constant ebb and flow of creative crashers—friends, family, and strangers who become fast friends—which is exactly as Channon and Bianca always pictured it. "Most weekends, it's like the cover of the Rolling Stones's *Beggars Banquet* around here," he jokes. "We've got three or four rigs parked in the front yard. We've got friends sleeping in the Airstream and teepee. Everyone's got kids, so we're barbecuing, camping out, and surfing. It's like a madhouse; an amazing, wild, perfect madhouse."

THE JIU-JITSU MASTER

There's a long (but little documented) history between the practice of Brazilian Jiu-Jitsu (BJJ) and surfing. Pros like Kelly Slater and Joel Tudor have been serious about the combat sport for decades. It makes sense that the same principles of leverage and execution used on the mat would translate to a surfboard. But, whereas most folks start out surfing and then find BJJ as a way to focus their technique, Shigeaki Tsubio came at it the other way around. He'd been practicing the martial art for seven years before a business partner convinced him to pick up a surfboard in 2011. "I fell in love instantly," he says. "The movement of surfing is just like Jiu-Jitsu; they both have a soft, gentle motion." It was his newfound obsession with riding that lured him from Tokyo to the coastal city of Kamakura, where he now starts his day in the water (sneaking in an afternoon session when he can) and ends it at his dojo, Carpe Diem, instructing all level of classes. "I wanted to establish a new culture of Jiu-Jitsu and surfing in Japan. It's existed on the West Coast of America for years, but it's new here," he explains. "Now, eighty percent of my students are also surfers, one even competes on a pro-level." At its core, this martial art is about gracefully avoiding trouble, not brute force, but Shigeaki admits (with a wink) that it's not a bad skill to have when dealing with localism in a lineup.

ACROSS Shigeaki alternates between two similarly sized longboards, this one by Joel Tudor and another (his favorite to ride) by Chris Christenson.
LEFT Japanese poet Matsuo Bashō is to haiku what Shakespeare is to sonnets. Monuments to his work, such as this street placard featuring a haiku that celebrates fresh bonito from Kamakura, can be found across the country.

MOUNTAIN HOUSE

Takashi and Misako Kumagai

Hayama, Japan

ON DRY LAND, TAKASHI KUMAGAI IS, BY HIS OWN ADMISSION, aggressive, unyielding, even argumentative. He's one of Japan's most well-known fashion photographers and stylists, with two high-concept lifestyle boutiques in Tokyo (CPCM in Harajuku and Wind and Sea in Komazawa) and his own menswear line called Naissance. He works as a brand consultant, a landscape architect, and a shop designer, with Saturdays Surf NYC and James Perse on his client roster. In other words, he's pretty adept at the art of multitasking.

But all that gets left on shore the moment he paddles out. "I am very easy and relaxed when surfing—even well behaved," laughs Takashi. "That's my true character, I hope." Riding is essentially his reset button, so he has no qualms about saying that surfing is the most important thing in his life besides family and friends. It's something he needs to do, and needs to do often. When the waves are working at Chojagasaki (a break five minutes from his house in Hayama) or Shichirigahama (a more popular spot a half hour west) he's there—not throwing tricks or hanging out with the "surf bros," but enjoying a nice, graceful ride and some solo time.

As improbable as it may sound for someone to fall in love with something that was essentially forced on him, that is exactly how Takashi's relationship with surfing began over twelve years ago. He was in Hawaii on a shoot. The crew goaded him into paddling out

ACROSS
Despite its reputation as a beach town, Hayama, which literally translates to "leaf" (ha) and "mountain" (yama), is enticing more and more creatives to relocate from Tokyo to its quiet, hillside community.

PREVIOUS PAGE, LEFT Takashi has an aversion to curtains, which is why you won't find a single one in his home. Instead, he installed double-glazed windows to help filter sunlight. **PREVIOUS PAGE, RIGHT** More jungle than garden, the outdoor space is a point of pride for Takashi, a place where he can happily while away a morning. **THIS PAGE** The basement shaping room is home to all things surf-related, where his quiver is filed away (in no particular order) and all his wetsuits and board-repair equipment are stored.

ABOVE Plans for an open-concept kitchen were scrapped in favor of a more traditional French layout, which separates the kitchen from the dining area—though they kept a subtle sense of openness by adding a panel of industrial windows between the two spaces. **ACROSS TOP** Most of the furniture in this home is vintage, not because it is collectible, but because it has a story. Takashi likes to picture the previous owners and how they lived with something that is now a part of his world. **RIGHT** The ebb-and-flow of items between house and shop is constant: Takashi will decide to let go of something and sell it at one of his stores, only to fall in love with it all over again and bring it back home.

at Diamond Head. And before he knew it, his frustration over
being pressured into surfing morphed into frustration over not
being good at it. "I think I was happy and surprised to have found
something I was into," he says. So he shaved off the dreads he was
rocking back then—they were too weighty when wet—and started
hitting the water on the regular, teaching himself to ride using the
good ole "monkey see, monkey do" method.

These days, he can't imagine his life without surfing. It's such
an ingrained part of his day-to-day routine. He's up at 5:30 a.m.
every morning, and if there is anything worth riding, he'll surf for
three or four hours before making the hour-long trek north from
his home in Hayama to his office in Tokyo. (If the waves are flat,

he spends that time gardening, his second favorite hobby.) He even has what he refers to as a shaping room at his house for repairing dings and scratches to his collection of thirty-plus boards.

Takashi's longish commute, incidentally, is very much on purpose. He keeps a strict separation between work life and home life, the distance acting as a physical barrier to his mental divide. He likes to joke that his mood is directly related to the air quality around him; the closer he gets to the salty sea breezes of Hayama, the more relaxed he feels. So the mountain-top home he shares with his wife, Misako, is meant to be a peaceful, Zen-like escape from the crowds of Tokyo—and a place for him to let his collector spirit run wild.

When you think of Japanese interiors, concepts like minimalism and feng shui may come to mind, the idea of less is more. But Takashi is a man of many interests and an accumulator of many things. When he was designing his home, for instance, he found inspiration in the organic modernist buildings of Finnish architect Alvar Aalto and the industrial-bohemian spaces at the Bowery Hotel in Manhattan. He has a thing for Native American culture and Northern European lighting designers. He collects T-shirts, Hawaiian necklaces, earthenware, stones, books, 303 surfboards (by friend and local shaper Kohei Chiba) . . . the list goes on and on.

If an item or a topic catches his interest, he disappears down a rabbit hole, devouring every fact he can find on the subject and buying things in twos or threes (or tens)—and his spaces are a reflection of that habit. He couldn't be less interested in having a picture-perfect room that tells a single story. Instead, he'll hang Moroccan pendants next to antler chandeliers, something functional next to something mystical. And though everything has its place and is expertly curated, nothing actually goes together in the traditional sense. But that fact, in and of itself, gets at the heart of Takashi's whole approach to design—and life, in general. As he would say: you should be you, no matter what that looks like.

ACROSS Reclaimed wood from a schoolhouse in the United Kingdom was repurposed as flooring throughout most of the rooms.

ABOVE Though he doesn't have a definable approach to gardening, Takashi does have a thing for acquiring rare and exotic plants.

ACROSS One of the many things Takashi inherited from his mother is this pendant light, which wasn't originally a pendant light but a woven sculpture made in the Tōhoku district where she grew up. **ABOVE** These wool tapestries are by his wife, Misako, who only started making them a few years back but is already selling them in a few major boutiques in Japan.

CRAFTY DOUBLE-WIDE

Sofie Howard

Paradise Cove, Malibu

YOU SURF TO LIVE. THIS CHERISHED NUGGET OF WISDOM WAS PASSED down to Sofie Howard by an old buddy she used to paddle out with in Malibu. "Surfing is the ultimate antidepressant. If I weren't out on the water all the time, I'd need Prozac."

Sofie comes from a long line of shredders and grew up on the water in Hawaii. Her dad put himself through medical school working as a lifeguard in Malibu and Venice in the fifties, and her uncle, Pork Chop—the only name he's answered to since the age of thirteen—was a local celeb of sorts back in the day who hung out with Miki Dora from *The Endless Summer* and was notorious for being a real hard-ass in the water.

When surfing is that much a part of your childhood, the lifestyle you adopt as a wave-loving adult is less weekend hobby and more second nature. Ask Sofie, for instance, how she can duck out of her Venice Beach office mid-afternoon because El Niño has kicked up some major winter swells, and you'll get a side-eyed glance as if to ask, "How could I not?" In fact, you'd be hard pressed to find someone more in sync with the day's conditions on the water than Sofie. Where most people turn to their calendars to plan their day, she's on Surfline like clockwork at 7 a.m. checking the live cams, tide tables, and wind direction.

But don't misinterpret her fluid scheduling tendencies as a sign of a surfer-slacker because that would be a mistake. Sofie's decades-long career is the stuff of music legend. She's an award-winning art

ACROSS
A lot of the design decisions for this house were made with surfing in mind, including the addition of this outdoor shower, which Sofie uses (in lieu of the ones inside) no matter the time of year.

NEXT PAGE
With a green-thumbed friend in tow, Sofie planted a small garden in front of her trailer using things like succulents that don't need regular watering. In fact, these have survived off of nothing but rain since going in the ground.

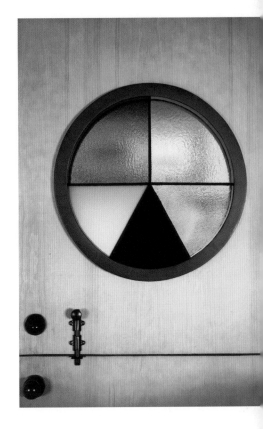

director who spent the early nineties at Geffen Records shooting some of the most iconic album covers of that era—Hole's *Live Through This,* Aerosmith's *Get a Grip,* and all the Nirvana albums from 1990 to 1997. She went on to launch Commune Images for Commune Design, before starting her own eponymous agency, where she represents new and established artists. Her work/life balance is enviable—and something she attributes to a laughably straightforward philosophy: "When the tide is right, you surf. When it's not, you work."

The kicked-back two-bedroom trailer she keeps in Malibu's now infamous Paradise Cove is mostly a no-work zone, though. When she's there, life revolves around surfing and hanging out at the beach—not that she could accomplish a whole lot given the cove's almost nonexistent cell reception.

She bought her first trailer, a small one-bedroom, seven years ago—back when Paradise Cove was still a semi-kept secret, not the sought-after destination it is today—and upgraded to the current "double-wide" in 2013. "It was a dump," she laughs, "one that screamed, 'I'm from the eighties.'" With the help of her then boyfriend, she gutted and revamped every square inch (inside and out)—all on a tiny budget and with lots of elbow grease.

ACROSS At her primary home, she has enough dishes to set a table for forty people. Here, she only keeps six of everything for the simple-yet-brilliant reason that "you limit the stuff, you limit the mess you can make."
ABOVE LEFT As an affordable (and so smart) alternative to hardware, holes were drilled into the kitchen drawers and adorable knotted rope handles were looped through.
ABOVE The front "hobbit" door was a gift from production designer/friend Steve Halterman who made the door and stained glass—which features the Navajo symbol for home— by hand.

CRAFTY DOUBLE-WIDE

Sofie chose three different fabrics for each of the mattresses on her sofa so she could switch them around at will. With the blue pattern on top it feels like a whole different living room.

ABOVE Hanging the accolades from her Geffen Records days in a prominent place felt too self-promotional. So, in a total wink-wink-nudge-nudge move, she mounted them on the walls of her tiny master bathroom.
ABOVE RIGHT The shower curtain was created by sewing a bunch of one-dollar bandannas together, something a seamstress was able to do for next to nothing.
ACROSS The only one who loves the beach more than Sofie is her best friend (and cuddle partner) Albert, who makes a beeline for the sand and water as soon as they arrive at the cove.

It's impressive how much she did (and how little money she did it with). The kitchen cabinets, for instance, are just whitewashed plywood with a butcher-block countertop. The curtains are burlap hung from iron hooks (each about a dollar to make). Some of the light fixtures were made using jelly jar shades and basic lighting parts, which only cost $8 apiece. Even the sofa, with its built-in plywood base and layers of mattresses, is deceptively luxe looking. "I'd say it feels like a proper beach house now," says Sofie, "built to withstand a tornado of sandy bodies." Which is the other remarkable thing about this 800-square-foot home: it can hold a crazy number of people.

"In the summer, I've got a houseful every weekend. I'm talking ten to fifteen people in here. We do beach bonfires. Make margaritas. Cook spot prawns. Being sandy and well fed is what this place is about. You know, two to three beers a day. Zero makeup. That's the vibe."

ABOVE In the guestroom, two twin beds can be wheeled together to make one king-size bed depending on the sleeping situation. **ACROSS** Little known fact: most trailers come with molded plastic ceilings, usually in a hideous beige. To mask the cheap material, Sofie covered hers in a dark blue that gives the illusion of painted wood panels.

ABOVE All of Sofie's boards were shaped by Donald Takayama. Most of her quiver is kept at her house in Venice, and then shuffled back and forth based on the swell situation. **ACROSS** Food is a communal event around here. Come dinnertime, it's not odd for folks to wander from home to home having a glass of wine, snacking on what everyone made to eat.

SPANISH CASA

Hana Waxman and Juan Muñoz

Sayulita, Mexico

THE FIRST EXPAT SURFERS DESCENDED UPON THE ONCE SLEEPY coastal town of Sayulita, Mexico, in the early 1970s. Back then, it was a tiny fishing village cut off from the rest of the country by miles and miles of jungle. Only the truly adventurous made the trek, arriving with nothing more than a surfboard and camping gear—some stayed for months, others never left.

Over the decades, the slow trickle of surfers to this town became a steady stream, thanks in part to the major highway that now connects Sayulita to Puerto Vallarta just an hour south. Today, it can only be described as a full-fledged tourist destination, luring artistic souls and newbie riders with its seasonal festivals and beginner-friendly breaks.

But back in 2006, when Hana Waxman first arrived in Sayulita, it was still clinging to some of its sleepy roots. Most of the roads remained dirt. You bought your seafood from a fisherman on the beach. A tombstone simply engraved with "Woody: Gone Surfing" was counted among the town's major sights. Like so many before her, Hana came looking for an adventure. What she ended up finding, though, was a husband.

"Not the journey I was originally expecting," laughs Hana, "but I met Juan in the plaza two days after I got here." Juan Muñoz, a surf photographer and property manager, had already been in Sayulita for two years at that point. The Nicaragua native planned to pass through town with a crew of pro surfers he'd been

ACROSS

No matter how crazy their day, Hana and Juan make it a point to get down to the beach every evening—if not for a surf, then at least for a walk.

NEXT PAGE

To achieve the indoor-outdoor flow that Hana wanted, she skipped glass windows and instead installed gorgeous shutters across the front of the house that allow unobstructed views of the water.

CARVE

documenting, but then, after realizing Sayulita was on the verge of becoming a surf hub in its own right, he never left.

The couple is now raising two young sons—Juan Costa, eight, and Joaquin Makai, two—in a little house that they're renovating. They can be at the beach in two minutes, in town in eight, and every night they fall asleep to a sound track of crickets and crashing waves. "Beautiful architecture isn't something this town is known for," says Hana, an interior designer. "So when you find a home with some character in a great location, that's a really good thing."

It was the original details of this Spanish-style house that caught Hana's eye—the traditional tile floors and roof and the high ceilings lined with wood beams. But like most everything else in the tropics, it had already aged well beyond its twenty years when they bought it and was desperately in need of a face-lift. Hana updated the bathrooms and kitchen countertops with a sturdy, stain-friendly polished concrete. They replaced all the windows with custom wood shutters and brought in new doors and cabinetry. "If you've ever seen the style of houses in Ibiza, that's what I was picturing: a lot of rock and wood, all very natural," she says.

The thing about design in Sayulita, though, is that it's much more about working with materials that can stand up to the heat, rain, and humidity than it is about personal style. Nice things are often delicate, and delicate things do not last in the rain forest—metals rust and fabrics disintegrate. That's why Hana chose to work with all local materials, even the furniture and textiles are locally sourced: antiques from Mexico City, furniture from San Miguel de Allende, textiles from Oaxaca. "Everything is clean, simple, and very shacky," she says. "We keep surfboards in the house and have a hammock in our living room. Nothing about our home is formal."

Technically speaking, nothing about their lifestyle is very formal. Cooking dinner is often done in swimwear, and certain family members have been known to go days without putting on shoes. But that's all part of the easygoing scene Hana and Juan wanted their sons to grow up around. Just about the only tradition this family never strays from is their Sunday routine: pack food, hit the beach, and surf till sunset.

ABOVE Along with his other multi-slash job titles, Juan is also a fisherman. He goes out at least once a week and brings home fresh catches like local red snapper.
ACROSS Coconuts are a daily part of this family's diet. They keep a pile of freshly chopped bunches on the front terrace for easy grab-and-go access.

Whether you set out to or not, sun hats are something that seem to accumulate when you live in a tropical setting. Hana turned her collection into a wall display in the master bedroom.

Living in Mexico and *not* owning a hammock wasn't something Hana could come to terms with. Since there wasn't space in their steeply sloping yard, she decided to hang one in her living room—like a loveseat only better.

Landscaping this steep property was a lesson in gravity. They chose sturdy native plants with deep root systems, so come rainy season things won't go sliding down the hill.

CHILL

the
lifers

FARMHOUSE ON THE BAY

Mark and Louella Tuckey
Clareville, Australia

ACROSS When the
weekend rolls around,
this family pretty much
lives on *Barny,* their
vintage timber cruiser.
The boat is actually
Louella's favorite place
to cook a meal.

IF A HOUSE COULD CHARM THE PANTS OFF YOU, MARK AND LOUELLA
Tuckey's happy-bright family home would render you trouserless. It
isn't that the rooms are so perfectly composed. They're not. Or that
the design is so spot-on trend. It's not. But everything about this
little 1930s farmhouse on the water is so quintessentially *them* that
you can't help but be sucked in by each and every eccentric
flourish—the kids' artwork–turned–kitchen backsplash or the
paper owl in flight above their sitting room.

Mark is a lifelong surfer, a teller of tales, and a maker of
furniture. His much-loved eponymous brand is known for its
simple, bespoke designs handmade from solid pieces of sustainably
sourced Australian timber. Louella, the company's creative director,
is a British expat with the heart of a stylist and the eye of an interior
designer. Together, their aesthetic is like the design world's version
of a call-and-response: her colorful, Mad Hatter tendencies wake
up and shake up his minimalist, clean-lined creations.

"Every single person that walks in says, 'OMG, this house is
so friendly,'" says Louella. "The whole idea, I think, is to have a
home that tells a story about your life, and if you're surrounding
yourself with what you really love, that can't help but happen."
For Mark, Louella, and their two daughters—Chilli, ten, and
Indigo, nine—that translates to a house that's jam-packed with
personality . . . and furniture. Mark's creations are mixed with a
collection of vintage Danish pieces. (They have a big soft spot for

ACROSS There's a story behind each work of art and every curated vignette. The paper owl, for instance, was a gift from Louella to Mark by artist Anna-Wili Highfield. **ABOVE** The surf culture Mark came up in was very environmentally active (to be a worthwhile human you helped the planet), which is why all his furniture is made from recycled or sustainably managed timber.

ABOVE Their library covers a myriad of subjects (architecture to music, surfing to motorbikes) all organized by color to add visual clarity to a disparate collection. **ACROSS** Louella isn't into retro vintage furniture; there's something so flimsy about it. But beautifully constructed Danish pieces, like these Børge Mogenson chairs, always catch her eye.

Børge Mogensen chairs.) There's also not a square foot of wall space that isn't crammed with artwork. Pieces by artist friends, like David Bromley and Mark Schaller, things the kids have drawn, tear sheets that Louella has pulled—it's all hung together, willy-nilly around every room.

Walking through the house feels a little like a tornado whipped through it and left everything ever so slightly (and ever so perfectly) off-kilter. Picture frames are knocked cockeyed. Coasters have never been and will never be something they own. In other words, their home is very relaxed, very lived in, and loved. "If the kids color too much on the table," says Louella, "we sand it off, no big deal." And that laid-back mentality, in a nutshell, is exactly the reason they live where they do, in a small flip-flops-and-shorts village called Clareville, in Sydney's Northern Beaches (minutes from where Mark spent his childhood), with the harbor as their front yard.

"We are out on the water more than we're inside," says Louella. They have a speedboat and a vintage 42-foot timber cruiser named Barny (their favorite place to entertain) docked in front of the house. In fact, the girls get to school most days by boat. "We have an amazing water life here," says Mark. "It's how I grew up, too. There was a lot of jumping in vans with friends and going up the coast toward Byron Bay. We'd tell our parents we'd see them in a few days, then sleep on the beach and surf at sunrise."

Mark likes to say he's a proud graduate of the university of life—and he has an arsenal of epic adventures to back that up. There's the story of how he and his friends used to pull the shark alarm at Noosa when the waves were working to get rid of the tourists. Or the summer he and those same friends made sandals from old tires and sold them at local markets to earn money for food, beer, and surfing. (Because what else does a twenty-one-year-old need?) In the early eighties, he met—and beat—Miki Dora at a game of table tennis in France, and then spent a few weeks surfing with him and his gang in Biarritz. Mark was even there when, in 1980, Simon Anderson first invented the Thruster, his three-finned surfboard design. Mark remembers he and a friend trying to explain, in a letter to their American surfer buddy, that the next revolution of boards had arrived.

In other words, Mark has seen and done a lot. And though it's tempting to chalk it up to luck (his friends often do) or a lifetime of being in the right place at the right time, Mark would disagree. "I think you kind of create your own luck if you put yourself out there. It's like surfing; you've got to paddle around to find the waves. Sit still, wait for them to come to you, and you'll miss everything."

ACROSS Mark has always been a bit of a gear-head. (He raced motorbikes back in the day.) This 1973 Ford F100 has been with him since 1989; the truck and $200 were the only things in his possession when he started his business. **ABOVE TOP** The skull-and-bones flag attached to the front fence was made by their interior designer friend Sibella Court. **ABOVE BOTTOM** In its previous life, this house was mint green. Painting it charcoal was the first task they tackled—and to this day, it's a rare week someone doesn't knock on the door asking the name of the color. (It's Domino by Dulux.)

FAMILY COMPOUND

Vanessa and Steven Alexander
Point Dume, Malibu

VANESSA ALEXANDER DOES NOT SURF. SHE CAN COUNT ON ONE hand the number of times she's ever even been on a board. But she's surrounded by a household of guys that do. So when the sought-after interior designer began the eleven-month gut renovation of her Point Dume home-slash-workspace, the surf lifestyle—and countering all the sandy feet, crumbles of board wax, and smelly wetsuits that come with it—was a big part of her vision.

"Let's be honest, no house is forgiving enough to stand up to three boys torturing it all day," laughs Vanessa, who picked materials for her Italian farmhouse-inspired home that look better with a little wear and tear knowing that her sons—Max, fifteen, Leo, twelve, and Jude, eight—would eventually leave their mark on every surface. The floors, for instance, are all reclaimed scaffolding, which came covered in paint splatters and plaster, so extra scuffs make no difference at all. A good shaking out every now and again is all it takes to keep her collection of vintage Moroccan rugs looking and feeling clean. And most of the marble she brought in for the kitchen and bathrooms is reclaimed, so, again, hard wear—not an issue. "I've never understood the precious approach to decorating, you know, rooms that look like no one has ever sat in them. I'm more about livability—and this house is very livable."

When she and her husband, Steven, a partner at ICM talent agency, decided to move their family out to Malibu full-time (instead of making the every-weekend trip from Pacific Palisades),

ACROSS
Surfboards are prized possessions around here, so Vanessa and her sons have come to an understanding: Most boards live outside, a few get to come inside, but none are allowed in bed (which was happening for a while).

THIS PAGE Vanessa has a wandering eye when it comes to beautiful photography. There are large-scale pieces all over the house, like Rosemarie Laing's "Car on Fire." **ACROSS** The entire kitchen was designed around this amazing island, which was created from two giant slabs of marble found in a Brooklyn bakery dating back to the 1920s.

ABOVE This sunroom-turned-television room was made for lounging. The built-in sofa is long enough to fit the whole family and deep enough that they can all lie down. **ACROSS** Vanessa will tell you that indulging in a glorious master bathroom is always a good idea; the fireside soaker tub is essentially her personal sanctuary.

having the beach as a part of their day-to-day life was paramount. It's how Steven grew up, in the water, surfing with friends, taking trips to Mexico or Hawaii. "We really wanted our kids to have that same experience," says Vanessa, though you could say they've wildly overdelivered on that aspiration.

Point Dume, their local beach, is a veritable den of pro-surfers. Max takes surfing as a class in school; it's his PE elective. So it's not an over-statement to say that the surf scene they are surrounded by is serious business. Most people aren't out there for the long, easy ride. They're digging in, throwing tricks, trying out new jumps. These kids are part of the next generation of Malibu riders; a lot of their buddies are looking to become either pro-surfers or pro-skateboarders.

"All the kids around here are sporty," says Vanessa. "They're just not into the typical football, baseball thing." Her house is actually across the street from the school, so most afternoons it's the first stop for her sons' legions of friends as soon as the final bell rings. But Vanessa has no problem with that; it's what the house was built for. Connecting the home to the yard, giving it an indoor-outdoor feel with lots of room for entertaining, was all part of the renovation plans. They tore down walls to create wide-open spaces and added skylights to flood every room with light. French doors, installed across the back of the house, connect the main floor to the clusters of outdoor areas: the backyard kitchen and edible garden, the pool and surfboard racks, and the soon-to-be skate park with a half-pipe and proper set of ramps and rails. "The property," she says, "has become our own mini-compound of sorts. It's a circus most days, but I'm enjoying the show."

ABOVE Getting to Little Dume is half the fun: a quick golf cart ride, followed by a scenic stroll down a wooded path, and you're there. **ACROSS** "Pulling more moves" sums up Leo's riding mantra, so he's working on his short-board game with his favorite thing to ride, a Fling by Superbrand (kept in his room, directly next to the bed, always within arm's reach).

END-OF-THE-ROAD HIDEOUT

Sean MacPherson and Rachelle Hruska MacPherson
Montauk, New York

ACROSS

This is a house folks can stay in with kids, dogs, even sandy, wax-covered surfboards without Sean and Rachelle ever worrying about things getting dirty or destroyed. In fact, most everything can either be hosed down or shaken out.

NEXT PAGE

Despite there being more than enough bedrooms for Dash and Maxwell to each have their own, Rachelle wanted them to grow up sharing one. It's how she and her sister were raised, and they're incredibly close today.

SO MANY THINGS HAVE BEEN WRITTEN ABOUT HOTELIER SEAN MacPherson, the tastemaker behind the Bowery Hotel, the Crow's Nest, and nearly a dozen other hot spots in New York and Los Angeles, that it's hard to believe the man has any stories left untold. If you've read even a single article about him you likely know that his parents met on the set of *The Endless Summer* and that his mother, Janet MacPherson, is a women's longboarding champion and a local celeb in the Malibu surf scene to this day. And you've almost certainly read that he's been "surfing since before he was born," a favorite story about how his mother rode while she was pregnant with him.

But what's probably one of the more fascinating things about Sean is that despite having racked up more hours than he could count on a surfboard over the years, he wouldn't necessarily call himself a "surfer." He is someone who has and does surf a great deal, but there is a subtle yet important distinction between the two for him. "Coming up in the 1960s and 1970s in Malibu, surfing was just part of life, an everyday experience, like the way New York kids play basketball," he explains. "Being a 'surfer' was not a cultural identity, like it is today. Not that that's a bad thing. We were just the opposite of that. We almost hid our surfing habit." In fact, it's an ongoing joke that, back then, whenever he met a girl, he never told her he surfed because surfers were the lowest things on the totem pole for most girls.

Rustic and exotic aren't usually design concepts you see together, but Sean and Rachelle have mashed up the two perfectly, setting off architectural details like wood planks and brick fireplaces with fabrics that add a super-bright punch of color and pattern.

Sean is of a different ilk; he's a different type of surfer from a different generation. Simplicity—in your ride and in your gear—is what matters above all else. "Growing up, surfing was this thing you didn't talk about, you just did it," he says. "You have a black wetsuit and a white surfboard, you keep your mouth shut, and you let your surfing do the talking." And little has changed for him over the decades. He still keeps his equipment nondescript (an Al

Merrick Thruster is his go-to), he still prefers a shortboard and a perfect right break (Malibu, Rincon, or Scorpion Bay), and it's still a very personal thing that he likes to do alone, at sunset, when everyone else has gone in for the day.

It was that stripped-bare, pared-down surf scene that brought Sean out to Montauk in the late 1990s; and specifically what sold him on the 1960s beachfront house in Ditch Plains that he now

Nothing about this little shack is taken seriously. Case-in-point: The boys' tub features a hand-painted dolphin mural courtesy of its previous owners.

ABOVE "Loungable" may not technically be a word, but it's a pretty accurate description of the cozy, plop-down-anywhere vibe happening in this house. ACROSS The stairwell is lined with photos of Sean's mother surfing. The shots go all the way back to the fifties, and include just as many from present day. NEXT PAGE Every weekend Sean and Rachelle have one goal . . . tire out the boys. It's a contest to see who sleeps the hardest (usually a tie between Sean and Maxwell).

shares with his wife, Rachelle Hruska MacPherson, founder of the digital media company Guest of a Guest, and their two sons, Maxwell, five, and Dashiell, three. "My one priority for the house was that I could surf without having to get into a car—that I could grab my board and go out on foot," he says. Back then the area was reminiscent of the Malibu of his childhood, a weird mix of rural and urban living side by side, generations of fishing families next to artists next to the few Manhattan expats that had made it out that far. And even though these days the Hamptons party scene has spilled over into this end-of-the-road hamlet, that, says Rachelle, is not their Montauk.

"Our lives are very busy during the week," she says. "So on the weekends, we don't make any plans; we just do what we feel like doing at any given moment." That often translates to long, luxurious lunches followed by family naptime. Their home is meant to be an antidote to their city life, a place that is connected to nature and comfortable without having all the luxuries of home at their fingertips. There's no television, no perfect Wi-Fi. It's a true escape, what they like to call their Robinson Crusoe fort on the water.

Even in the face of a recent renovation—which included the addition of a new, open-concept, second-floor living-dining-deck space—the home still feels very rustic, simple, and cozy. The walls and ceilings are wrapped in reclaimed barn wood. Textiles they've collected from around the world (like throw pillows from Saudi Arabia, rugs from Morocco, and tapestries from India) are layered through all the rooms. Live-edge walnut countertops are mixed with vintage appliances in the kitchen. Overstuffed seating calls to you from every corner.

In spite of the thoughtfulness with which this home was put together, neither Sean nor Rachelle would say they're necessarily attached to a single thing in it. "In a weird way, our furnishings are sort of like beach towels," says Sean. "The ones you buy are always missing, and you always seem to have someone else's. Things come and go; we try to let it be and just enjoy the experience."

THE SHAPER

Riders tend to fall into one of two board-buying buckets: those happy with a mass-produced pop-out and those who believe in the artistry of a hand-shaped surfboard. Neither is right or wrong, to each his own. But if you're of the latter school of thought, then Chris Christenson is a name you know. That's because where most shapers are hyper-focused on a handful of board styles, Chris shapes everything . . . well. His design approach is twofold: he studies the decade a particular style of board was popular, and then applies what we know in the present to that model. "Take the end of the longboarding era, '66 and '67, that's when they started refining the equipment," he explains. "I approach my longboards as if 1966 never stopped . . . where would that design be today?"

Chris started his shaping business in the early nineties out of his dorm room. He spread the word by papering the campus with flyers, took orders on his answering machine, and created a makeshift workspace by tossing extension cords out his third-floor window and using a set of desk chairs to make a shaping bay. Two decades later, his factory in San Marcos, California, makes close to two thousand boards a year, though he still attracts (mostly) the same sort of rider—the serious sort. "My best customer is the guy with the shittiest car," he laughs. "They'll spend more on boards than their car is worth, take off to Indonesia for six months, and come back sunburnt and smiling." That's what he wants for his boards, for them to be ridden—not turned into artwork. As he puts it: "If in eighty years one of my boards that was never waxed sells for more than one that was, I'll be in the room calling 'bullshit!'"

This exact spot, Bolsa Chica in Huntington Beach, California, is where Chris's dad took him to catch his first wave when he was eleven years old.

COTTAGE IN THE COVE

Mel Hayhoe and Drew Down
Avalon, Australia

IF YOU SURF AVALON BEACH, YOU KNOW WHO MEL HAYHOE IS. SHE'S as ingrained in the surf culture of that community as *Surfing World,* the country's longest running surf magazine. She's also one of the few folks living along the twenty-mile stretch of coastal villages known as Sydney's Northern Beaches who can call herself a local; her family moved there from England when she was three years old, and she's been there pretty much ever since. And even though most days you're more likely to get her chatting about her aversion to the "kale smoothie-ification" of her town than the almost thirty years she's spent in the surf industry, Mel does, in fact, head up one of the largest surfboard distribution companies in all of Australia and Asia.

Mel and her partner, in life and business, Drew Down, have run Onboard Industries since the eighties, when it was originally called Insight Surfboards, and they work with some of the most well-known shapers around: Al Merrick's Channel Islands, Thruster inventor Simon Anderson, Haydn Lewis, and Catch Surf. They have two shops in Australia—one in Mona Vale, the other in Byron Bay—with an additional outpost in Bali. But what's even more impressive—and the thing, according to Mel, she is proudest of—is the work they do with their surf teams, especially at the Super Grom and Pro Junior levels. "We are sponsoring a lot of girls these days, which is really exciting. There are so many more surfing now—many from here that are fun to watch, like Holly Wawn and sisters Cedar and Bodhi Leigh-Jones."

ACROSS
This yard was once overwrought with foot-high lantana bushes and had no clear path to the front door. It took ten weeks to weed the yard, lay down the lawn, and hand-place every stone.

ACROSS Like most houses of this era, this one had teeny-tiny windows originally placed with airflow in mind, not views, something Mel remedied by installing bi-fold doors opening to a veranda (essentially her outdoor living room). **ABOVE** Some say a blue porch ceiling wards off evil spirits, others think it deters insects from nesting, but Mel just loves the color. In fact, she loves it so much she left it intact when she walled in the porch to make a sunroom.

ACROSS What's now the dining room was essentially the whole of the original home. Today, it feels like an extension of the backyard, with its wood paneling, grass-green rug, and outdoor furniture. **ABOVE** Propped along the top ledge of the wood paneling are a handful of Mel and Drew's favorite records, which include everything from obscure surf film soundtracks to classics like Jimi Hendrix and The Cure.

ABOVE Mel cooks a lot, and often for a lot of people, so she wanted a kitchen that was simple and functional. She designed this layout herself by mixing and matching IKEA pieces. **ACROSS** The vintage workbench was rescued from a house up the street. They were throwing it out and Mel spotted it, popped some glass on top, and now uses it daily for food prep.

ABOVE These shells-on-string have seen many lives. They're an op shop find Mel had up for years before getting tired of them and packing them away. Some time later, she rediscovered them, and now they're one of her favorite things in the house.

ACROSS Mel measures the greatness of a ride by how fast she paddles out for the next one, "when you're barely off a wave and your first thought is 'again,' you know you're having a good set."

Mel's house is just as much of a rendezvous point—for family and friends, for friends of friends, and for vagabond surfers—as the shop in Mona Vale. "I constantly have people over," says Mel. Her tiny beach shack, with its indoor-outdoor flow and low-key vibe, is definitely inviting. But, frankly, the real draw is the yard itself, which is less lawn and more Pacific Ocean, and happens to be home to one of the best breaks in North Avalon. "Even when I'm not there, people stop by and hang out."

Her niece and nephew pitch tents in the garden and camp out with friends on a regular basis. Every Tuesday, kids from the school down the street (the same one Mel attended) take over her yard for gym class, otherwise known as "surfing sports." She even

has an open board-borrowing policy: "We always keep a few under the deck. People come by, take one, bring it back when they're done." And at low tide, practically everyone living in her little cove is out with a glass of wine or a beer floating in one of the natural pools that form along the shore. "I don't plan parties, really. They just seem to happen," she says. "One person comes over, someone else stops by, before I know it I'm making dinner for twenty people."

But she wouldn't have it any other way. Her the-more-the-merrier spirit has been the way things are done at this house since it was originally built in 1916. Or so says Mavis, Mel's ninety-two-year-old neighbor, whose family built the home and was among the first to settle in Avalon. Back then, it was one of fewer than a handful of little fishing cottages in the area that wealthy families used to trek out to in horse-drawn carriages from Sydney. Over the years, of course, Mel and Drew have made changes—an outdoor porch became an indoor sunroom, they added three bedrooms, and they blew out a wall and replaced it with bifold doors that open to the sea—all done on an as-wanted basis, which means the house feels slightly puzzle-pieced together in the coolest, quirkiest way. Case in point, a few original outdoor windows now look into the affixed bedrooms.

But whenever the choice comes down to adding a modern convenience or not losing something charmingly original, Mel has always picked charm. It's the reason the chipped blue ceiling paint in some rooms has never and will never be touched, and that the wood paneling gets repaired instead of torn out. And, in truth, the cobbled-together floor plan suits her magpie tendencies just fine.

She is a self-proclaimed collector of anything and waster of nothing—and the things she shares her home with tell that tale. There's a colorful collection of outdoor seating parading as dining chairs. A bunch of rusty old wash bins she found in the house when she first moved in are now planters in the garden. A trove of op shop (the Aussie version of a thrift store) treasures fills every nook, cranny, and shelf. In other words, this fishing cottage-turned-surf shack has always felt like home to Mel. "I kind of knew the first day I saw this house, ten years ago, that I was never going to leave it. I seriously don't think I ever will."

ACROSS This little guy is Peanut; he came to Australia from New York City for an extended stay with a photographer friend of Mel's, and, well, he just never went back.
ABOVE When the frangipani trees are in bloom, you know summer has arrived. The flowery scent washes through the whole cove.
NEXT PAGE Mel had serious doubts about this home after her first peek inside; the woman who lived in it before her kept rabbits . . . in the house. But then she saw the view out the window and thought, "I can do this."

CENTURY-OLD FIXER

Dave Muller and Lana Porcello
Outer Sunset, San Francisco

CALL IT FATE, KISMET, OR SHEER BLIND LUCK, BUT SOMETHING aligned in the stars the day Lana Porcello and Dave Muller found their dream home. Dave, on his way back from a surf session at Ocean Beach, started chatting with a woman carrying boxes out of a house just three blocks from the water. Lana, at their warehouse loft in Oakland, came across a listing on Craigslist for a "cozy little cottage" and immediately began speed-dialing its owner. It wasn't until later that day that they realized they were both in real estate lust with the same house. One month later, they moved in.

That was 2005. Their trek to Outer Sunset came hot on the heels of the opening of the first Mollusk Surf Shop, owned by two buddies of theirs who had been actively recruiting them to the neighborhood. Back then the area was still a very sleepy coastal inlet with not much going on. "Mollusk was kind of the pioneer," explains Lana. "They opened, and then ding, ding, ding—so many other small businesses popped up." It's been one big game of follow-the-leader ever since, with young artists and local surfers slowly trickling in and opening coffee shops, design stores, galleries, and, in the case of Lana and Dave, a farm-to-table restaurant called Outerlands in 2009.

It's hard to believe—given the buzz around Outerlands—but opening a restaurant was never a goal for this couple. It happened fortuitously, like the best sort of happy accident. "When we first got out here, if you weren't surfing, you were hanging out at Mollusk,

ABOVE Almost every inch of this house, inside and out, was created using salvaged materials (a lot of it repurposed redwood fencing) and leftover materials from their restaurant renovation (like the new front windows).
ACROSS Dave's quiver is stashed in a locker alongside the house, and includes (mostly) boards by shapers he has a relationship with. There are a few Andreinis and Mandalas, a Chris Christenson twin keel, and a Renny Yater longboard. **NEXT PAGE** A couple of greenhouses were among the first additions to this ever-growing mini compound. The "yard" is sand, so having any sort of garden requires aboveground planters.

ABOVE "Anti-furniture" is how Lana would describe their design approach. They prefer custom built-ins (with tons of much-needed storage) that they can then make their own by adding blankets, pillows, and a few decorative accents. **ACROSS** Lana raided the Heath Ceramics overstock tile section for the house. The upside of that was huge savings; the downside is you don't necessarily know what you're getting. She pieced together this patterned backsplash completely by eye.

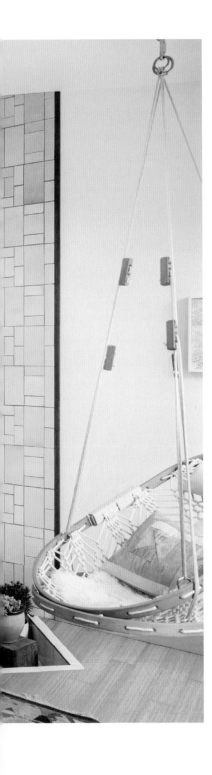

sometimes all day, because there was no place else to go," says Lana. Eventually, those hangouts trickled over to Dave and Lana's, and epic—almost weekly—dinner parties ensued. "I don't know how we made the jump from hosting dinner at home to opening a restaurant," but eight years later, their neighborhood hot spot is a local institution, drawing in foodies from all over San Francisco and Oakland.

Even with the restaurant a few blocks away, their home is, and probably always will be, a gathering place, not because of its size (it's only about 700 square feet), but because there's just something so dreamy about the teeny-tiny space. It's become a joke among their local friends that inauguration into the neighborhood requires a stay in the guesthouse.

There's no official paperwork documenting the history of Dave and Lana's home, but they think it was built in the 1890s, a suspicion based on a penny from that era they upturned in the walls during one of many renovation projects. They also believe it was most likely never even meant to be a primary home. "At that time, people didn't live out here," explains Lana. "But if you came to the ocean a lot, you would often build a little swimming shack to have a place to keep things. That's probably what our house started out as."

ABOVE Tucked away in the front corner of the property is a small art and music studio for Lana. The (rare) downtime she ekes out for herself is spent nurturing her drawing and singing practices.
ACROSS Leithian's lofted nest of a bedroom sits directly above Dave and Lana's bed. The little stained glass window connecting the two is not just a window, but a delivery slot for Leithian to drop surprise "gifts" for her parents.
NEXT PAGE This is a television-free household, so family time means activity time. They do everything from reading to cooking to gardening together.

Over the years, they've been pecking away at updates to the property, adding on two lofted bedrooms for their kids, Leithian, eight, and Aman, three (yes, those are Tolkien references), and constructing extra outbuildings (a greenhouse, a laundry room, and a surfboard shed) as needed. They also rehabbed the kitchen, living room, and bathroom with the help of handy friends and lots of salvage materials.

They went in expecting a certain amount of unknowns, as one does when renovating a building from the nineteenth century. But the things this couple has seen are laughable. They found carpet installed directly on sand, no subflooring whatsoever. A storage loft they slept in for years, it turned out, was "floating" without any structural support. And the kitchen walls were nothing but pieces of plywood tacked together with steel wool. It was as if the only thing holding this home up was its sheer will to exist. But, Dave and Lana say, they've learned a lot—mainly that steel wool was the duct tape of the 1890s, and that they have some pretty fantastic, and helpful, neighbors.

This sense of community, with its all-for-one mentality, extends to the water, where, even though Ocean Beach is the only place to surf in San Francisco proper, you will not find a lot of aggressive localism. That's due in part to the fact that it's a beach break, so you're hunting waves instead of sitting in a lineup, and in part because the swell situation is just so hit or miss. "When it turns good, you have to be ready for it," says Dave, who has been surfing since his early teens, "and if you live across town, you're probably going to be too late." So by default, the local surfers have all become a tight-knit crew. "I think it's a very special situation, the way we get to know each other and our experiences in the water together," he says. "I've been out there with a group of friends and surfed with dolphins underneath a rainbow. That stuff happens here . . . and it just feels like magic."

MODERN BEACH HOUSE

Paul and Liz Masi
Amagansett, New York

PAUL AND LIZ MASI MIGHT BE THE ONLY PEOPLE IN HISTORY WHO have figured out how to make family vacation photos fun for nonfamily members. Instead of awkward smiles in front of watercolor sunsets, they keep what is essentially a highlight reel of Paul and his two sons (Evan, twelve, and Kyle, eleven) shredding. And, as awesome as those rides are to watch, what makes these moments even more warm and cuddly are the cheers coming from Liz and their nine-year-old daughter, Hope, behind the camera; it's enough to give you secondhand surf-stoke.

Being out on the water is something this family rallies behind. It's a factor in almost every major decision Paul and Liz make. Vacations are surf trips. They follow the Rip Curl Pro like it's the Super Bowl. It's even the reason they live where they live. When Paul, who owns the firm Bates Masi Architects, had the option of moving to Manhattan or Long Island after graduate school, they chose Amagansett to be close to the water, to have the sort of outdoorsy lifestyle they both grew up with.

Paul is one of those rare people who has been surfing in Montauk since the seventies, back when it was still predominantly a fishing village, and he was one of maybe three other people in the water. His first friend as a kid was the son of the owner of Sunwear, the only surf shop in town at that time. "The whole family lived in the rear of the shop," says Paul. "I'd sleep over, like every night all summer, and his dad taught me to surf." By the

ACROSS
Don't expect to find a single *Surfer's Journal* in the little den-slash-family library; those are snatched upon arrival and meticulously organized by number in Kyle's room (perusing permission is required)

NEXT PAGE
Windows across the front of the house would compromise Paul's well-designed acoustic barrier so he installed an incredibly long skylight in the main room instead.

ABOVE Most of the artwork in the house is by Paul's father, who is a painter. The elder Mr. Masi has been creating Japanese-inspired scenes using ink on rice paper since the early sixties.

ACROSS In the master bathroom, Paul has what he refers to as his winter shower, which is inside, and his every-other-season shower, which is outside (though the series of sliding glass doors that separate the two are almost always left open).

eighties, their surf duo had turned into a proper surf crew, with a bunch of local teens splitting their time between the water and the half-pipe Paul had built in his parents' yard. "None of us played football. We didn't play baseball or soccer. We surfed and skateboarded nonstop. That was our life." And this crew of "misfits" is still intact today—surfing together regularly in between busy workdays.

That's the sort of lifestyle Paul and Liz wanted for their kids, one where they are outside more than in, and the friends they make in elementary school could very well be the friends they have

as adults. So the modern cedar-plank-clad home that Paul designed for the family was always meant to facilitate those goals. They purposely built close to Amagansett's main drag (and, by default, the train tracks) so they could walk to everything. The kids' school is one block away, and they're ten minutes from the beach. But, even though they wanted to be close to town, they didn't want it to *sound* like they were close to town.

To control noise, while creating an indoor-outdoor vibe, you could say that Paul took a "business in the front, party in the back" approach. (Quite possibly the only instance that that phrase is

ABOVE The hope was to build a home that weathered well, so there's no paint or stain on any of the materials—the wood is meant to gray and the metal is meant to rust.

ACROSS All the cedar planks, inside and out, are held in place not by screws or nails, but by metal fasteners connected to inner cement walls. This allows the wood to expand and contract with the season without splitting the boards.

meant and can be taken as a compliment.) The front of the house, the side closest to the main street, is a series of three twenty-inch-thick cement walls, placed in ascending order, that create a sound buffer over the yard. The back of the house, in contrast, is almost all floor-to-ceiling glass. The main living space opens out onto the pool area via a set of massive sliding glass doors, which tuck neatly into the walls. Most of the year, with the doors open, the backyard simply feels like an extension of the house itself.

Though they live in a summer destination, surfing isn't something they reserve only for the summer. This family is in the water year-round. In fact, their definition of the perfect surf day involves a couple of inches of snow on the beach and a nice February swell. "The winter scene is so much better out here; the waves are bigger, there are fewer people," Paul says. "I'll take the kids before school, catch a dozen waves, drop them off with wet hair—is there anything better than that?"

Paul has always loved surfing.
But once his boys started riding,
seeing the joy they get from it at
their age, made him love being
in the water more than he ever
thought possible.

ACKNOWLEDGMENTS

This book would not have been possible without the help of friends, friends of friends, and people who were willing to help out a first-time author simply because. Every home was discovered through a wonderful process of social connectivity that harnessed the power of community. I am deeply thankful to all those involved.

To the wonderful people featured, thank you for letting us into your beautiful homes and allowing us to capture a glimpse of your remarkable lives. Your stories have been profoundly inspiring to me—and now, I hope, to the world as well.

I could not be more thankful to Heather Summerville, who was a true partner in the making of this book. Your extraordinary ability as a storyteller and your devotion to the creative process have been astounding. Your experience and expertise were indispensable. I could not have done this without you.

The incredible talent of our photographer, Brittany Ambridge, made this book what it is. Your honesty and hard work energized the entire project. It was a privilege working with someone who cares so much for her craft. And a big thank-you to Stephanie Fosnaugh, who made each photo as beautiful as it could be.

I would like to thank Angelin Borsics at Clarkson Potter, who took an extraordinary chance on me. To think, all it took was one breakfast, and we knew we could create something beautiful together. Your dedication, your trust, and your insight were the forces that took this book to the next level.

A huge thank-you to the tireless efforts of the experts at Clarkson Potter: Jana Branson, Kevin Sweeting, Stephanie Huntwork, Joyce Wong, Kelli Tokos, and Kim Tyner. What an amazing experience it has been working with such professionals.

A special thank-you to Liz DeCesare, at Authentic Media, who pushes me into new territory every day—and just simply believes in me.

To Bryn Schuyler and Kristin Marino, from Haus Interior, thank you for helping with the big stuff, the small stuff, and everything in between. You are what kept business running as usual at Haus Interior, and I am very grateful for everything you do.

To my parents, who provided me with the confidence to take on this project, I could not be more grateful. Your unconditional support in everything I set out to achieve has been the most loving gift you can give a daughter. You have always been my motivation. I love you both.

I lovingly dedicate this book to my husband, Mike, and to my son, Wolf. Mike, every day I feel so grateful we found each other. You are truly the most amazing husband and father. Your patience, humor, and support mean everything to me. Wolfie, I am so lucky to be your mother. You are already such a remarkable little boy. I love you both more than words can express.

And finally, to the design community: What a beautiful world we live in, where we are inspired every day by one another's craft, creations, and creativity. Thank you.

NINA FREUDENBERGER received her BFA and bachelor of architecture from Rhode Island School of Design before launching a career in interior design. Founder of the boutique design firm Haus Interior and a line of nationally distributed Haus candles, she lives with her family in Mar Vista, California.